BLUE WILDERNESS

Ron & Valerie Taylor

The Cousteau shark cage stands at ninety feet over the edge from the world-famous Con Shelf at Shaab Rumi reef in the Red Sea.
Once used as protection against sharks, this man-made structure has been reclaimed by the sea and is now part of a living reef.

In the world of the undersea arts, couples are rare. It is as if the compounded rigors of exploration and cinema or photography demand a degree of devotion that leaves little time or energy for others. It is a world of private visions pursued by dedicated loners.

Valerie and Ron Taylor are the triumphant exception.

They are a true team, each complementing the other's talents to produce films that possess a magic and a message far more indelible than either would be capable of alone. In films, photographs, writings, and personal appearances, their love for the sea and for one another merge to create a perfect synthesis of art and life.

Theirs is no empty virtuosity. Two deeply caring individuals, Valerie and Ron are constantly reaching out to sensitize us to the beauty and the plight of our nonhuman fellow travelers on this planet. Whether the objects of their fascination are sharks or corals or dragons, Valerie and Ron continually manage to win our respect for the needs of other species. They are especially committed to educating young people, the inheritors of our world, to appreciate and protect the natural treasure we enjoy.

It is an honor for me to contribute a preface to this beautiful work of art, as it is an honor to consider myself a friend of its authors. I have followed their journey with admiration and affection, and am gratified that their work touches the lives of so many people in such a positive way.

It takes a special fortitude to swim with great white sharks, as Ron and Valerie do on a regular basis. But they seem equally at home in the unfamiliar waters of publishing, displaying perhaps an even deeper courage in allowing us to know them intimately, to share their inner lives. Thus readers of this book have a unique opportunity not only to discover a world of wonder and light, but to meet a pair of passionately creative devotees of the ocean realm.

Jean-Michel Cousteau

10   In The Beginning

20   The Flowers Of Life

30   Fish Stories

52   The Filming Of Blue Water White Death

64   Komodo

80   The Australian Sea Lion

90   The Filming Of Jaws

104   Saving The Potato Cod

112   The Great Shark Suit

134   The Shark Repeller

We dedicate this book to the great adventurer Michael Ian McDowell,
who took Ron and me with him to unexplored reefs
in far-flung oceans.
We thank you, Michael, for your companionship
and affection.

BLUE WILDERNESS

FOURTH DAY PUBLISHING, INC.
Post Office Box 6768
4067 Broadway
San Antonio, Texas 78209
210-824-8099
210-820-3522 fax
oceanica@eden.com

ISBN: 0-9642736-9-1
Library of Congress Catalog Card Number: 95-061626

Printed and bound in the United States of America.

First Edition

No digital manipulation has been
used in the reproduction of the photographs in this book.
All incidents described and/or pictured are true and factual.
Interaction between divers and sharks should
be considered highly dangerous, and
no attempt should be made to duplicate the actions
or situations described herein.

A percentage of the profit from the sale of *Blue Wilderness*
is donated to Oceanica, a non-profit organization
dedicated to the conservation of marine ecosystems,
and the protection of marine biodiversity.

The ocean holds a fascination for us all. Some, like myself, are completely captivated by its wonders; others merely touch the edges, the subtle mystery of this other world that calls to the soul of their being. Bright windows of memory cut the hazy images of a distant childhood. My first balloon, my first kitten, and strongest of all, my first glimpse beneath the surface of the sea. I see it now: that plain brown kelp, flirting with my imagination as it flowed weightless with the surge. It seduced with a promise of unknown things; it was the beginning of a love affair that has not dimmed with time. The promise continues, never-ending, reaching beyond the limits of knowledge into a thousand lifetimes yet to come.

In The Beginning

I have traveled the world underwater and have come to see the earth as a living thing, and the sea as both its lifeblood and the source of all life. After spending over four decades underwater, often in situations others would see as risky, I can say that I have never considered myself to be either brave or stupid, just fascinated. Fascination has a way of leading one on.

When I was a child, most of the world had been climbed, walked over, scaled, sailed across, and mapped, but the sea was right at my doorstep and it remained a mystery. How do you end up with your arm in a shark's mouth over and over again? What path leads a young woman to spend much of her adult life underwater, in the company of all manner of marine animals? You have to be able to recognize opportunity and grasp it in both hands. Then, (at least in my case) it simply happens, unfolds—one adventure after another.

The events of childhood tend to push each of us in directions we don't see at the time, only recognizing them in retrospect. In my early life, my father managed a battery business and my mother kept house, looking after me and my two younger brothers. Although I was a poor student, I loved school and was considered an excellent athlete. At age eleven, I had the good fortune to get a job looking after a boy with club feet, a two-year-old. I took him walking in his stroller for two hours a day—at least that's what his mother thought. But I would hide the stroller in the reeds, put him in the basket on my bike, then ride off to join my girlfriends. We would have a grand old time. My friends and I treated this boy like a living doll, and he loved it. I'd take him to the beach, have him sliding down hills on cardboard, and bring him back to his mother filthy but happy. His mother trusted me, the little boy loved me, and I adored him, for I was busy learning from him what only children can teach.

When I was twelve, I had infantile paralysis—polio. There was no way I could realize the seriousness of what I faced, for I would not see my family for three weeks, and it would be two years before I saw the last of my illness. Through it all, I never doubted that I would have a complete recovery, for at the age of twelve you simply accept that you can do what you have to. The experience became a turning point in my education. Experience teaches well, for polio left me willing to persevere, no matter how difficult the situation, a useful trait for an underwater photographer.

Before my illness, my mother had sent my brother and me to Sunday school with the Brethren, because their school was nearest to our house. The Brethren didn't believe in makeup, music, movies, singing (except hymns), or dancing, but they did believe in helping others, and they did it with a grace and intelligence that marked my life. During my hospitalization, books from the Brethren began to shape my future. They sent me the classics: *Black Beauty, Treasure Island, David Copperfield, Huckleberry Finn*, on and on, little books with tissue paper pages between covers of dark blue or dark red cloth, with gold lettering. Here was adventure. I couldn't believe there were so many possibilities in the whole world. So I read like a lunatic, and still do to this day. I love Huck Finn and have read the novel perhaps fifty times. That book became a moving force in my life because Huck showed me that you should never pass up a chance, that you have to grab an opportunity, for it might never appear again. I envied Huck's freedom and the great adventure his life became.

At fifteen, I went to work and became self-supporting. Because I could trace figures and had a steady hand, I found work at the New Zealand film unit as an animator. Soon after, my family returned to Australia. We lived in a house on the water. My brothers and I knew so little about life in the sea that it was as if we were the first persons ever to discover the wonders of the marine world. As fortune would have it, the man next door was a ship's chandler, and one day he gave us a scuba tank with a regulator (backpacks, pressure gauges, and the like were not available), a sample that had been sent him from America. We had no one to advise us about the dangers involved, so we began making ten-minute shallow dives. It was probably our fear of the deep water that saved us from the consequences of our ignorance.

In Australia, I soon found work drawing comic strips for a Press Feature Service, and continued to turn out drawings for *Buggsy Bear*, *Foxy Fagan*, and *Li'l Abner* over the next ten years. It was easy work, I could do it quickly, and, for a woman, the money was good.

A young Australian named Ron Taylor had begun shooting a few news clips on sharks in black and white for Movietone News. His footage showed these monsters of the deep being hunted, and theater audiences would cheer every time a poor wretched shark thrashed away

I was twenty-four years old when I saw the reef. My first piece of coral, fragile as gossamer, spread delicately around the bow of an old wreck. I floated in awe of its delicate beauty, reluctant to move away. I was looking as a child looks at all new things, my mind soaking in the image, locking it away for future reference, learning by sight what no words, no matter how beautifully written, can teach. Age does not limit the ability to learn by observing. It is the right of the young and the privilege of the old; it is the key to understanding, and in the realm of innerspace, it can unlock the door to a treasurehouse of knowledge that never ends.

In 1970 I planted small pieces of colored coral in this pool on the southern edge of Heron Reef. Every time I visited Heron Island I would walk to the reef edge and check how my corals were coming along. This photo and dozens like it were taken in November 1979. Two years later a cyclone filled the pool with rubble and it was completely destroyed, which is a shame because I was proud of my pink corals growing so well, and curious to see if they would eventually cover their end of the pool in color.

its life on the end of a spear. About age twenty-two, I met Ron at the St. George Spear Fishing Club in Sydney, and I soon became his underwater model, swimming around in front of his camera like (I thought) an Australian Esther Williams. We started working together, and I fell in love with the lifestyle: with going to isolated places, the adventure of it, the spontaneity, the action, the struggle, the sheer possibilities for the unexpected. Ron and I married, and led a hard but adventurous life. Movietone News continued to buy Ron's 16mm film on sharks, which they would blow up to 35mm and show in the newsreel theaterettes, helping our budget tremendously.

The immediate focus of life then was simple: getting enough money to survive. We would live in a tent on the beach, going out in our boat and shooting film underwater in the morning. Then in the afternoon we would spear fish and sell them to the other campers for petrol money. Sometimes, if we were lucky, we would swap fish for meals at a nearby restaurant. Chinese restaurants were the best and most generous. As we acquired enough good footage, Ron would edit the original film on a twinroller editor with a magnifier and a splicer.

When we first started showing films, we had to do voice-over narration every night, which became very tiring. Going from town to town, with our companion John Harding, we would sneak around putting up posters to advertise our films. The police caught Ron one night and made him remove every poster. He didn't finish until early morning and never went putting up posters again. We would hire barns, theaters, halls, whatever we could find that could be used as a theater; it was a wild, haphazard way to make a living, and what happened above water was sometimes as unexpected as what happened below.

I recall reading Hans Hass's *Diving to Adventure*. Hans was a gorgeous man and the first great underwater photographer. His wife Lotte was a fine diver, and their adventures were amazing. I wanted to be just like Lotte Hass. Looking back, I can see that I was.

The wonders of the coral reef are easily accessible to people of all ages. I searched for a picture that illustrated this by image alone. Heron Island, on the southern end of the Great Barrier Reef, is an ideal place for this type of photography. At low tide the reef flats surround dozens of tidal pools, perfect for snorkellers and reef walkers alike. Ron used a 15mm lens when he took this picture of me watching a snorkeller from the edge of the coral. The shot was planned in detail beforehand, even to the girl holding a piece of dead coral. I particularly like the reflections on the surface of the pool.

Any money we made was immediately swallowed up by the cost of more film, but we earned a living, bought a better car, and invested every spare penny in fuel for the boat and better cameras and lenses. We were always thinking of ways to publicize our film shows without spending money. We gave away tickets on radio shows, brought out shark fighter tee shirts (Australia's first), and orchestrated stunts to attract crowds to our films. One trick was to cut a dead shark out of the mesh nets, put a spear in it, and pull it up on a beach where there were lots of bathers. This attracted a crowd and a few lines in the local paper, but we didn't do it often. We made a variety of films, and Ron started to win international awards for his photography. He had now transformed from a champion spear fisherman into a cameraman with a unique sense for capturing just the right action. In the early 60's we did an hour black-and-white special called *The Shark Hunters.* Ron said we'd made our shark film, and now we had to go on to filming something else. Perhaps it was just as well that we were blind to our future, for it probably would have been impossible to plan what followed in the next few decades.

We were young and free. In those days there was not much of a market for underwater photos, and publishers were not much interested in fish pictures; they wanted sharks, preferably with people in their mouths. I never made a conscious decision to make a life out of diving with cameras, but it was Ron's dream. It was never easy, but one thing simply evolved out of another. The turning point was when Peter Gimble invited us to participate in the filming of *Blue Water White Death*. From there on we were asked to do the filming of sharks in the wild for a variety of feature films, of which the latest, *The Island Of Dr. Moreau,* saw us working with tiger sharks in the open ocean. Over nearly four decades, our work with sharks—particularly great whites—became a way of life, one that I am still enjoying. The ocean has been good to Ron and me. We still follow its liquid path, for to us it is the elixir of life, and we have been fortunate indeed to have tasted its wonders.

It's a special thrill to take a child diving. They do exactly as they are told and believe in you completely. The young boy in the picture is my nephew Jonathon, who was ten years old, meeting his first shark. Overhead the sea was very rough. A current was running at around two knots, so it was not an ideal situation even before we started. On reaching the bottom at forty feet, we had to crawl over the rocks into the shark gutter. I expected him to give up as soon as he felt the current and was very proud when he battled on. On meeting his first shark, Jonathon remarked to his sister, "It was terrible getting there, but seeing the sharks made it all worthwhile." These are sharks who were, until thirty years ago, considered to be maneaters. Isn't it amazing what a little education can do?

Released from gravity's burden, these divers drift as one with the lifeblood of a liquid world. The sea makes us different creatures—silent, weightless, and amazingly graceful. We can soar like birds or float like thistledown. Intoxicated by the exquisite freedom of flight, we are absorbed into the essence of our existence, that mysterious place we call the sea.

These young Pacific bottlenose dolphins were born in captivity. I took this picture during the making of a television commercial in which one of them, Tuffy, starred. To my surprise I discovered they were completely untrained, and had little contact with humans. I was even more surprised to discover that I was supposed to train them to ring a doorbell and swim into a house when the door was opened. At first it seemed an impossible task. The reward of food didn't interest them, but I noticed that they loved to play with a rope quoit. I joined in their game and found that by playing hide and seek with the quoit, I could persuade them to do anything. By holding the quoit behind my back when I opened the door, I had Tuffy swimming into the hall and looking as though he was talking to me, when actually all he was doing was looking for his quoit. All this took place in bone-chilling water in South Australia.

Ron and I have spent over forty years exploring the marine world, forever seeking the rare and beautiful for our films and photographs. Sometimes the magic just happens. Other times it needs a little help before the picture in our minds appears through the lens. But no matter how it happens, the satisfaction of seeing the longed-for image glowing on the light box never diminishes, and the elixir of success feeds the desire to do better next time, no matter what hardship or frustrations stand in our way.

The Flowers Of Life

We air breathers who only visit the water briefly give the creatures of the sea too little credit for their sophistication. Most marine animals appear to humans to have no consciousness, no sense of time, no particular personalities. It has been my experience, however, that closer acquaintance with various marine life forms suggests other possibilities.

I started as a spear fisherwoman; for ten years I hunted fish as a sport. During this time, I was constantly learning about my quarry; I came to see different personalities in some members of the same species. For example, at Heron Island bommie, Harry the eel behaved differently from Fang the eel. One fat grouper would be shy, another much more assertive. Because we understand so little about how eels, groupers, and other marine animals communicate and perceive life, the easiest way to deal with our ignorance is simply to dismiss them as dumb beasts, moved solely by instincts. Now after decades of diving all over the world, working with marine animals in dozens of documentaries, I see them a little differently.

Some creatures have a way of holding a mirror up for humans, and if we pay attention, perhaps in the small marvels that they show us, we can learn a little more about both them and ourselves.

Decorator crabs, for instance, design their camouflage from materials around them, but on close examination, each seems to have its own distinctively arranged costume. Whether the crab dresses for protection, a better chance at a meal, or in hope of a sexual encounter, we probably will never know for sure. Different members of the same species of crab dress differently in the same waters. Given that most humans aren't sure themselves just why they wear what they do, we probably should not expect to learn what motivates a crab. The differences that divers see in forms of crab camouflage, however, suggest that each crab expects to gain some advantage out of its particular spongewear or seaweed costume. While evolutionary camouflage often gives marine animals a better chance at survival, the decorators appear dissatisfied with their natural appearance and shop for an altogether different look from the one evolution has given them.

Perhaps there is more to their decoration than we humans understand, for each crab has its own sense of fashion, and crabs have been known to change decoration. Whatever the individual crab's sense of style, each presumably chooses its particular camouflage to yield results. While fashion designers, culture, the weather, and economics all influence how humans dress, we are still waiting to learn what explains the small mystery of fashion among decorator crabs.

In the early 1970s on Komodo Island in Indonesia, I came upon another small marvel. The nutrient-rich waters supported life more abundant, and more diverse, than anywhere I had ever seen. The warm tropical water here mixes with cold currents rising from below, leaving the sea literally bursting with marine animals of all sorts. Brilliant corals carpet the rocks; millions of bright fishes course through their branches. Crinoids of every hue flower in the currents; ascidians of blue and white and orange and pink and yellow cling to the rocky outcrops. They produce a feast for the eye and wonder at nature's diverse abundance. Where most marine environments have only a subdued vibrancy, Komodo is a changing kaleidoscope of fairyland color.

A rainbow bouquet of ascidians, sponges, soft corals, and algae shimmers in the water at Pink Sand Beach, Komodo Island, Indonesia. This is marine life at its most exquisite. As the animals grow, the delicate arrangement will change, the strong overpowering the weak, until the bouquet is no more.

Our friend marine biologist Jack Randall theorizes that this place near the junction of many waters—Indian Ocean, Banda Sea, Timor Sea, China Sea, Philippine Sea, Pacific Ocean—could be the place from which modern marine life springs. Here, he suggests, may be where the creatures of the sea fled during the encroachment of the last Ice Age, which made habitat impossible for them except in small areas around the equator. Today, probably as a result of cold upwellings, many temperate zone inhabitants have remained trapped as the ice receded toward the poles.

With the amazing abundance of life, the problem for the sedentary marine creatures around Komodo is simply finding a place to rest, somewhere to sit. It took Komodo, with all its overcrowding, to help me see some small outposts as a different form of underwater civilization, what I call the posies. Caught up in the pursuit of more dramatic marine inhabitants, I was first somewhat slow to see these shy animal clusters. They had always been there, but I had never looked at them closely, or given them much thought.

Posies are actually small groups of various animals that for all the world look like a flower arrangement. My first posy I found quite by accident when I developed the film of a series of nudibranch shots. There in the background lay a magnificent miniature garden, a natural arrangement of animal life that collectively held a beauty and character distinct from everything around it. I was so taken by what I had ignored for so long that I began to look for similar small arrangements. Over the years, clustered in secret places, under ledges or hidden among larger organisms, I found these tiny groups of delicately balanced animals glowing in their own little worlds of harmony and beauty.

A closer look at a posy revealed a complete society, a whole world on a small scale: tunicates, shrimp, ascidians, algae, anemones, polyps, hydroids, sponges, sea squirts, starfish, and a host of other marine creatures. Collectively some six to fifteen creatures will find an out-of-the-way patch of dead coral where the current regularly delivers dinner. To the naked eye, it was as if nature had taken out her palette and brushes to create a small living painting.

The more I looked at them, however, the more I learned, and soon, with the help of a magnifying glass, I would watch a dreamy cast of characters, most of them tiny fish, shrimp, or crabs, emerge and go about the business of everyday life. Virtually invisible to the naked eye, larvae like minuscule lice would move through the animal forest. Tiny shrimp, less than a quarter of an inch in length, would flit nervously in and out, while fish half the size of my little finger would sit waiting for something edible to arrive. It was as if twenty or thirty different forms of life had found a peaceful coexistence in this small universe. Despite years of learning to photograph marine animals, I would find myself so fascinated by this minute world that I would sometimes spend a whole dive without taking a single shot, watching things I never dreamed existed.

Examining posies closely and photographing them became sort of a personal obsession. Visiting the same little posies of animal life, year after year, I found that there were no really good large posies. Animal harmony of the kind I sought had a natural limit to its scale, as if the survival of these little societies relied on a silent collaboration among creatures that competed for the same living space.

It appeared to me that the whole symbiosis of a given posy would be put at risk when one or two creatures—usually the hydroids and ascidians—began to get out of balance and take over. The other creatures would soon disappear, and the dominating survivors would eventually claim sole occupancy of the real estate. Slowly but inexorably, however, these victors in the competition would pay a high price, for they would in time outgrow the space. As they slowly fell into decline, a new generation of polyps, sponges, shrimp, and anemones would resettle and gradually create an entirely new posy.

In its own way, the behavior I see in posies reflects the history of all life. At some point an individual or a group begins to win the competition for control. The careful balance between self-interest and communal interest which up to this point worked now begins to unravel. Sooner or later, more for the few becomes less, as the victors begin to suffer from size and age. In this tiny world unto itself, the rise and fall of the delicate web of survival comes to mirror the common experience we share in life.

Delicate marine bouquets of ascidians, stinging hydroids and algae, and three white nudibranchs with their lovely coils of yellow eggs are as beautiful as any floral bouquet.

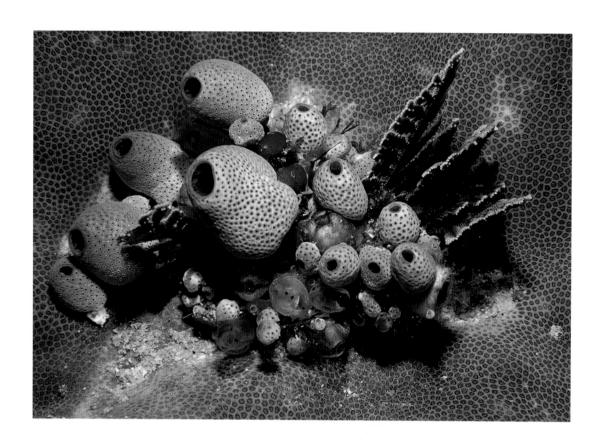

The Pink Sand Beach on Komodo Island supports the richest, most diverse little coral reef I have ever seen. This tiny triplefin sits on a bouquet of marine animals that rival any man-made flower arrangement, yet to the little fish it is the whole world, and it will probably never know another.

Oblivious to the beautiful animals surrounding it, the lined nudibranch below feeds happily on what appears to be a stinging hydroid.

Opposite, a lovely chromodoris nudibranch grazes in a field of algae, growing over an orange sponge. Sprouting among the algae are fine, hairlike stinging hydroids.

Similar in radial symmetry to terrestrial flowers in the spiny choke family, a beautiful but toxic fire urchin, to the far right, is in itself a complete bouquet. This spiny creature, a nocturnal feeder, usually spends the daylight hours tucked softly away in the corals, though I cannot imagine any predator brave enough to tackle all those sharp, venomous spines.

Nudibranchs or shelless mollusks are among the most colorful and bizarre of marine inhabitants. How they manage to find members of their own species amongst the vast array of invertebrate life on the reef has always amazed me. Found worldwide, these fascinating small creatures are seemingly endless in their variation. The vibrant purple-and-yellow cluster above, photographed on Banda Island, Indonesia, was busy doing something very secret at the base of a feather star.

Also photographed in Indonesia, the two nudibranchs at top opposite seem to be feeding on what appears to be a patch of brown algae at the base of the soft coral. Following the leader, or perhaps more accurately, tracking a chemical trail, the four at left were found in the Arabian Gulf.

Fish Stories

When I look back on it, there are a handful of experiences I've had in the sea that have shaped how I think about all marine life. Each involved getting to know creatures individually, being able to recognize one marine animal's face and behavior as distinct. A few of these experiences have left me with a sense of the character of marine life that science seems to ignore, for occasionally the best of human qualities seems to appear in creatures we often dismiss as just fish.

While we were working on the thirty-nine-part television series *Barrier Reef* in 1970, the producer supplied a huge barge to hold our two-person submarine, our generators, and other necessary equipment. We had to train the local fish to be natural around the actors, who were required to appear completely at home in the sea, so we spent long hours underwater each day becoming used to each other. Early in the series, we found that a school of thirteen kingfish had taken up nightly residence under the flat hull of our barge. Like us, they saw the barge as a refuge, and their presence became a pleasant part of our daily lives.

Each morning when we would move the barge to our regular underwater location, the kingfish would leave to go hunting. When we returned to our anchorage each night, our fish would be waiting, pleased to have a secure night's lodging. One morning, about three months into the shoot, we noticed a one-meter kingfish with a huge bite out of its stomach. Some predator had left it partially crippled. Unable to move well, it now became easy prey, and we pretty much agreed it could not survive.

When the barge was moved to our filming location about half a kilometer away, we were amazed to see the kingfish had followed us. Swimming weakly, the wounded fish moved under the barge, a healthy kingfish shepherding it. The sick fish positioned itself against the small keel, then, quite deliberately, its comrade took up protective residence in front of it. When I tried to approach the wounded kingfish, its protector would block my path by positioning itself between us. When we returned the barge to its evening anchorage that night, both the fish followed, with the stronger appearing to protect the weaker.

Each day the barge would move, and with help from a comrade, the wounded fish would follow. Each night, a reverse migration would be repeated. It was obvious that the fish felt safer near the protective shadow of a human presence. Even more remarkable, each day a different healthy kingfish would appear and stand watch over the sick one. Although they knew I was not a danger, I was never allowed to feed or get close to the wounded fish. During several weeks of this kind of watch-keeping, the wounded kingfish gradually recovered. Scales grew over the hole in its side, and then one day we moved the barge, and to our delight, all the kingfish vanished, their weakest member now ready to leave shelter for the hazards of the open sea.

Kingfish have a kind of courage that divers appreciate. Instinct should tell a fish to flee when a predator wounds another in the school, but kingfish appear to go on beyond that kind of limited behavior. It comes as no surprise, really, that a number of kingfish would override instinct to protect and help a wounded fellow, and that as a group they would share in the task of providing daily protectors. Divers know that if you spear a kingfish, its companions will often try to bump it off the spear. The others, trying to help, will follow the speared fish right to the surface. Humans, it seems, have no monopoly on courage or loyalty, above water or below.

Famous conservationist and painter Sir Peter Scott called fishes "birds of the sea." His favorites were the butterflyfishes. He claimed he could tell how rich a reef area was by the number of different butterflyfish species it supported. This saddleback butterflyfish was photographed at night near Heron Island, Great Barrier Reef.

Not only do different fish have contrasting characteristics, but fish of the same species can also have personalities that differ from one to the other. For example, while parrotfish are extremely fussy about where they sleep, returning to the same spot night after night, their sleeping habits can be surprisingly diverse. Some back into snug holes; others will wedge themselves sideways under a ledge of coral. The longer I observe fishes, the more fascinated I am by the choices they make and the diverse personalities I meet among them. It's very rewarding, observing fish and their different lifestyles.

At night these three parrotfish look to be happy sleepers. Some even have smiles on their funny little faces, almost as through they are having a lovely dream.

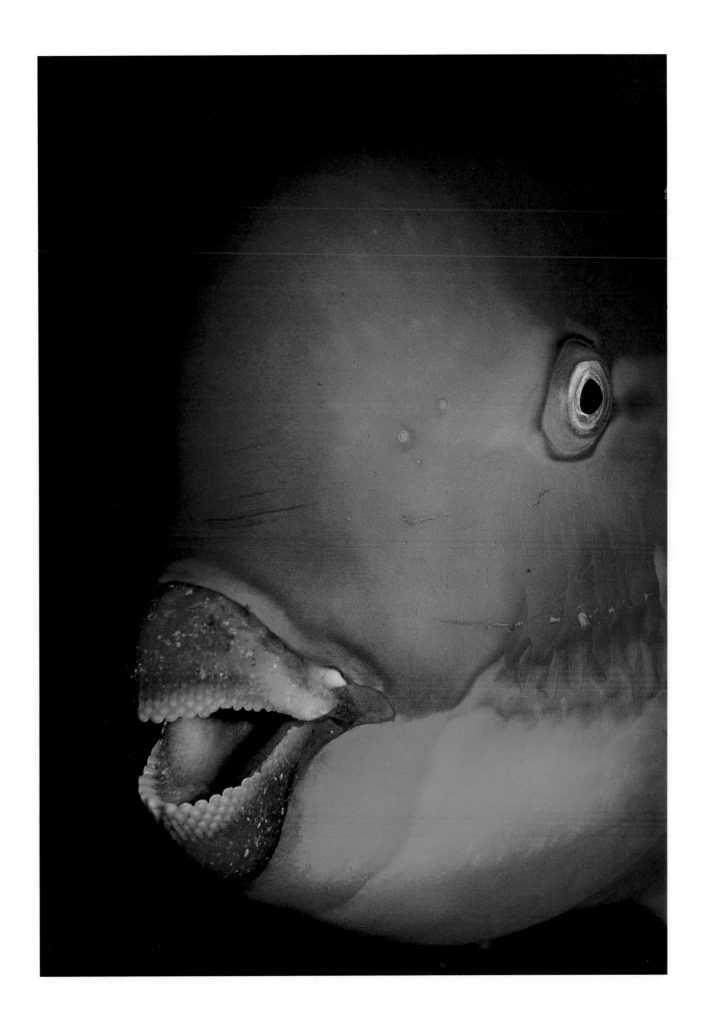

Cleaning is big business on the reef, and numerous small fish, shrimp, and even juvenile fish get a meal by ridding their hosts of parasites. Even triggerfish, some species of which will attack anything in defense of their nest, put their aggressive behavior aside to take advantage of the services of the cleaner wrasse.

I have seen shrimp cleaning fish many, many times, but only once have I been lucky enough to get a good picture. This tomato rockcod allowed nothing to disturb it; not even my flash could make it flinch.

Shimmering like silver dollars, schools of batfish are found throughout the Indo-Pacific. They move as one through the water, a curtain of life flying on invisible wings across the liquid skies of innerspace. Their appearance fills the mind with fleeting wonder, and all who see them feel pleasure with their passing.

Crocodilefish, like so many of their cousins in the flathead family, use camouflage as an aid to hunting, though it's not often they snuggle into soft corals as this one has. The fish above lives off the Pink Sand Beach, Komodo Island, Indonesia, and is an old friend.

Easily photographed, harlequin tuskfish are pugnacious little wrasses with strong individual personalities and incredible curiosity. Watching them has given me hours of diving pleasure.

n the Indian Ocean, the isolated coral island of Europa boasts only a herd of goats and a little stunted vegetation they have yet to eat. It is a lonely island, and it was there that I met a turrum in need of companionship. Darwin had a deep grasp of the workings of nature, but to my knowledge, he had never made any personal acquaintance with a marine creature, an experience that is missing in his much-publicized view of life. I was spearfishing when a huge turrum, a member of the jack mackerel family, swam straight toward me from a considerable distance. As it neared, I raised my loaded speargun, but the fish swam right up and bumped its nose on my spear. I was flabbergasted; I realized that I could never kill a fish that behaved so personally.

As I swam away, the fish fell in beside me. We moved in unison across the reef, as if we were twins joined at the hip. I could not have followed this fish if I tried, but for reasons of his own, he had decided to match my every movement. Then I saw Stan Waterman with his 35mm movie camera, and I swam over to show him my new friend. As I stroked the belly of this friendly fish, it was clear that here was an old turrum, one probably near the end of his days, his fins a little ragged, his mouth battered. Perhaps he had outlived his friends, but he seemed altogether happy to have us as his companions.

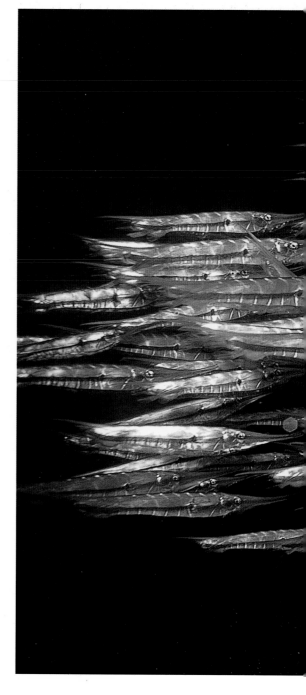

The turrum swam around, looking at Stan as he filmed, then he decided to suck in my ponytail—which he soon spat out all over my face, discovering, I suppose, that my hair was not for lunch. Ron arrived with some pieces of fish, and the turrum, sensing something good to eat in the vicinity, attacked Ron's snorkel vigorously, nearly pulling it off his face mask. Frustrated by his failure with the snorkel, the turrum began to look about in agitation. When I offered him a piece of Ron's fish, the gift was immediately accepted. My majestic, big-eyed friend proceeded over the next half hour to gulp down Ron's entire catch, as if playing with divers and acting for the camera were something he had done all his life.

I was delighted with my new friend until he tried to gulp down my fishy glove; I watched horrified as my hand slowly disappeared into his mouth. A tug of war began between us. Fortunately, I was able to work my hand out of the diving glove, which was held on by a wide rubber band. The fish appeared to be having some difficulty swallowing the leather glove, but the rubber band slid down nicely. *

We were amazed by the fish and very pleased that Stan had gotten it on film. Ron's gun, which I had left on the coral, had somehow disappeared. As we swam the area searching for it, my friend the turrum again swam with me in easy unison. I now kept my hands carefully tucked under my armpits—not that I was scared, but one leather glove would make a terrible mess of my friend's digestive tract, and two would probably kill him. I didn't want that to happen.

Eventually, I realized that we were nearly out of air. As I swam away, it occurred to me that I had moved from being someone ready to kill this fish to someone now worried about his future, and it had been the friendly behavior of the turrum that had caused me to change. To the turrum, I was a strange creature, but apparently a harmless and suitable companion until he could find one of his own kind. I often think of that fish, for there is no place in the sea for the sick, the unwary, or the old, and clearly he needed a friend. No wild land animal, in its natural state, would have shown such trust. For a brief time, I was privileged to share a little life with him, and without understanding, he simply accepted me for what I was, a fellow traveler in a wide sea on a small planet.

Fortunately, the following day, we found my glove on the coral where the turrum had left it.

Normally these strange shrimpfish are found quietly hanging nose down among whip coral, so imagine my surprise when I came across this group swimming along like any other school of fish. I followed for several minutes, hoping to draw ahead and get a second shot, but they quickened their speed to match mine. It seemed as though they had a definite plan. Maybe their soft coral home had died and they were looking for a new one, or perhaps they were just out for a swim. Who knows, but I love my one shot of the traveling shrimpfish.

Of course, not all fish faces are beautiful; some of the most interesting belong to intriguingly bizarre species that are perhaps even more fascinating in their habits than are the more commonly recognized reef fish. In a fast move for a frogfish, the yellow fish at right has just captured a meal: note the eye of the unfortunate prey still clearly visible inside the frogfish's mouth.

Peering from his hole, this fat-lipped frogfish waits patiently for his next meal to pass. It could be a shrimp or some other unsuspecting marine creature; it doesn't matter to the frogfish, who will snap it up with lightning speed.

Under an old army jetty near Ambon, Indonesia, is an area of amazing animal diversity. The giant frogfish, opposite, is one of four different species of frogfish I found living among the jetty's pilings.

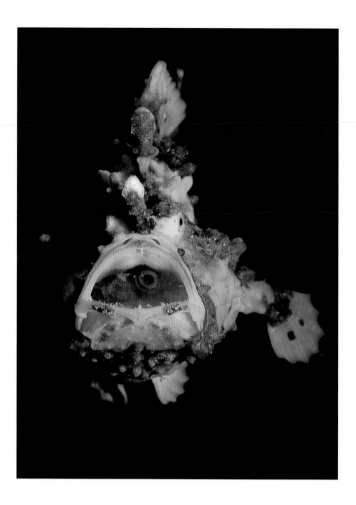

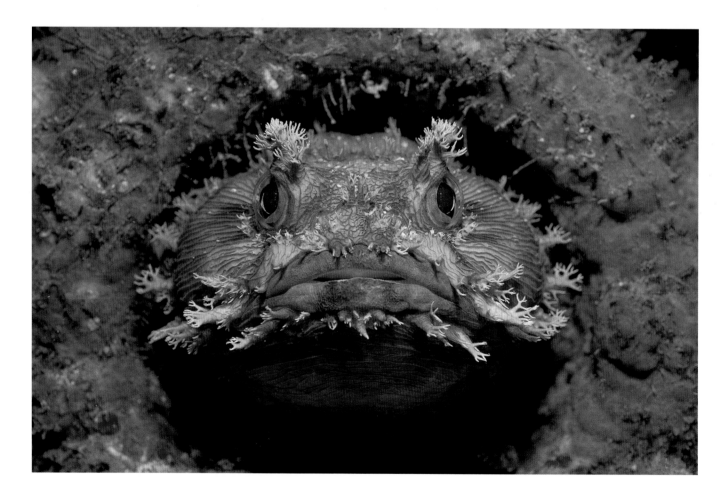

The scene was the Coral Sea, forty feet down in a sandy gutter on a coral reef, in midafternoon during late winter 1972. Ron and I were on scuba, and our assistant, Vic Ley, was snorkeling. We were after Coral Sea sharks for a television documentary. Because our baits had attracted none, Ron signaled Vic to spear a fish. We had learned in our spearfishing days that nothing attracts reef sharks faster than the panicked vibrations of a wounded fish. It was a strategy we had used to attract sharks for our photography many times in the past.

Two large turrums appeared, swimming together as they so often do. Curious about us, they had moved out of deeper water for a closer look, their flat, silver-gray bodies making a perfect target. Vic's spear penetrated one of them high on the back just beneath the dorsal. After a few stunned seconds, the turrum dove for freedom, tearing free of the barb. The fish fluttered to the sand, where it shuddered crookedly toward the reef, its companion swimming frantically after it. Within seconds, three whitetip reef sharks appeared. To our amazement, the healthy turrum shepherded the wounded fish into a narrow cave under a coral ledge, then covered the entrance of the cave with its body. Here was a pelagic fish, one which normally never stops swimming, but it lay almost motionless in front of the cave.

The sharks knew where the wounded fish was, but at first they dashed around as if confused. All of us now hoped that they would take our baits, but instinct impelled them to pursue the injured turrum. The wound in the fish had drawn the sharks, and there was nothing we could do. Eventually the sharks pushed their way behind the lighter turrum, and tore its bleeding comrade apart. The survivor swam around for a moment, as though searching, then slowly it turned away and disappeared into the gloom.

It was one of the saddest things I have ever seen underwater. Later Vic Ley, a professional diver, said, "Valerie, I'll never spear another turrum as long as I live," and neither of us ever has. Right this moment, I could draw the scene in fine detail, and even as I write, the feeling leaves me saddened at what we unwittingly did.

Others can say it was only a fish, but here was a fish prepared to use its own life to defend a comrade against overwhelming odds. That it failed only made the moment more of a lesson. It is a piece of my past I will not forget, this sudden death and defeated act of courage in the sea.

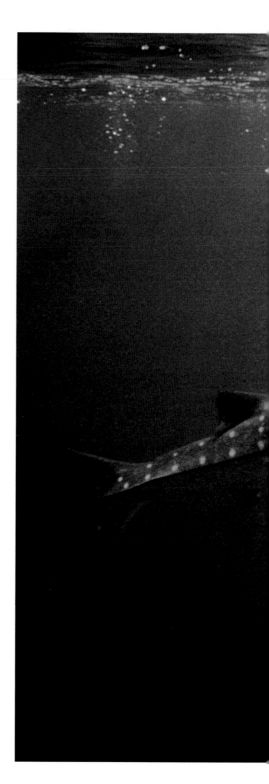

As tiny as a thimble or as enormous as several school buses, the wondrous fishes of the ocean realm are found in an astonishing variety of sizes and shapes. Feeding solely on minute planktonic organisms, the biggest fish in the sea, the whale shark, is the gentlest of creatures. Among the smallest, a shy juvenile tomato clownfish peeks out from its protective home of anemone tentacles.

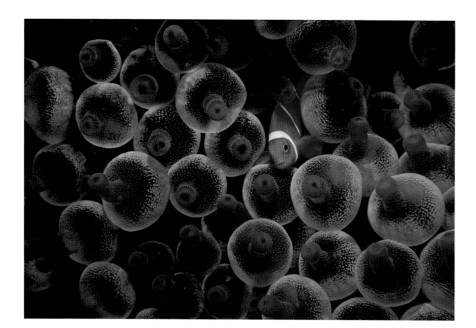

I met this cheeklined maori wrasse at Shaab Rumi in the Red Sea. It was just there quite suddenly, very close. The fish hung in the water and looked me in the eye, changing color constantly. I managed to take these shots before it drifted away. Perhaps he was cross with me, or maybe I was in his territory, but I felt a definite annoyance in his attitude.

Pufferfish are usually solitary animals, and it was indeed a rare treat to see a school of these comical-looking fish hurrying along the reef top. Why they had congregated and why they seemed to be in such a hurry is anybody's guess.

Normally difficult to approach, this beautifully marked Dussumier's surgeonfish seems to become more relaxed around sunset when this picture was taken.

This photograph of the unicorn surgeonfish, Naso brevirostris, with its marvelous elongated horn, was taken at Raine Island on the Great Barrier Reef. Like all surgeonfish, they have a rough, abrasive skin, which is very popular with the woodcarvers of Papua New Guinea as a sandpaper for finishing off their carvings. During the day, they cruise the open water along the reef edges, coming in at night to sleep among the sheltering corals.

Below, male (smaller of the two pictured) and female ghost pipefish hang together among the branches of a black coral. Until they hatch and can swim free in the water, the eggs are carried in an extended stomach pouch. The male cross-fertilizes them while they are in the pouch, leaving the female to carry and care for his offspring.

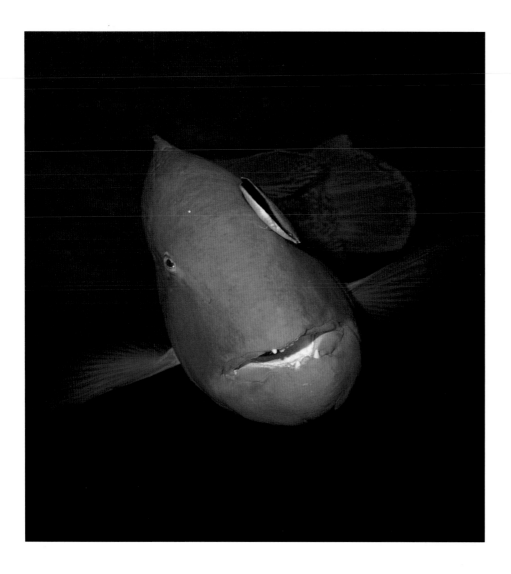

The black tuskfish pictured here with a cleaner wrasse lived at the Heron Island bommie. Old scar-face, we knew him for years. The only time I could photograph him was when he was being cleaned; otherwise, he was too flighty to approach. One day he just disappeared. I guess even fish can die of old age.

Delicate and flighty, a baby batfish, Batavianus platax, *is barely three inches high.*

There are three types of fish I simply cannot resist photographing: lionfish, clownfish, and barracuda. I find I can really work with them in almost the same way I work with a model, and they are all so wonderfully photogenic. I visit this group of old friends, a school of resident barracuda, each time I visit Papua New Guinea.

The Filming Of Blue Water

n April 1969, Ron and I began what was to be one of the most exciting two days we have ever experienced. Had the events that I wrote about not been substantiated by that wonderful film *Blue Water White Death*, they would appear unbelievable. Looking back, it all seems incredible, but at the time it was our daily life. We were following the whaling fleet out of Durban, hoping to film deep water sharks when they came to feed on the harpooned whales. To Ron and me, it was the highlight of the six months we spent working on the film.

In *Blue Water White Death*, the great white sharks were considered to be the stars, but to us it was the oceanic whitetips which caused our most dangerous and exciting moments. Even now, twenty-six years later, I can still close my eyes and fill my mind with that purple void, full of gray torpedo shapes circling, ever circling, and our cages like empty webs, dangling lifeless as the whale.

The dead whale floating in a cloud of blood, my companions, dark, awkward figures surrounded by the elegant beauty of a hundred sharks. Our whale catcher, the *Terrier VIII*, silhouetted on the surface far above.

I can see it all as though it happened yesterday. Each of us was driven there by a different need. I was not afraid. I wanted the excitement, the exhilaration of flinging myself into the abyss of the unknown. I did what my companions did, even though I felt that in doing so we could possibly be killed. The intoxication of the moment was all-consuming. It left no place for fear or misgivings. For me, it was the ultimate adventure.

The men with whom I shared this experience I loved. We were welded into one by trust and faith, and I still think of them often with the affection and respect that can only come from sharing a profound experience.

I consider myself to be lucky, and my life richer because of this adventure. It was quite simply the highlight of my diving career, and I would do it again tomorrow and pay for the privilege.

It was late April, some eighty miles off the South African coast, in the Indian Ocean. The wind had been dropping away, and the sun was emerging as a morning squall passed. About three weeks earlier, Ron and I had set out from Durban on the *Terrier VIII*, the rusty, greasy, foul-odored South African whale catcher that now labored beneath us. We were waiting for the weather to clear. Along with Peter Gimbel and Stan Waterman, we had been filming oceanic sharks feeding on the harpooned whales left floating in the wake of the whaling fleet. Although each of us had considerable experience with sharks, at the time we did not realize the impact that our dives over the next six months would have. The shark scenes in *Blue Water White Death* were to become the turning point as to how divers would react when confronted with dangerous sharks in the wild.

The steel hull of the *Terrier VIII* stretched beyond a hundred feet, its sides low in the water for easy access to the harpooned whales, its bridge high and open to offer a clear view of the gunner and his quarry. During rough weather, of which we had a great deal, the decks were awash. In the bowels of the ship an immense steam engine rumbled, the throbbing of its great

White Death

Taken by Ron in 1967, this picture and a series of six others were the first underwater stills of a white shark ever to appear in print. Ron took these shots by hanging off the poling platform of a tuna boat, filming the white sharks as they came in to the baits. This shark and four others were caught by game fisherman Alf Dean during the making of a documentary called Hunt for the Great White Shark. Alf Dean taught Ron and Rodney Fox how to attract great whites for filming. Photographed at Dangerous Reef, South Australia.

pistons sounding for all the world like an angry superheated heart. During storms, to reach the front of the ship where we ate, we had to take the catwalk that passed above the engines. The heat was indescribable; I would look at the crew, stripped to the waist, skins glistening with moisture, and wonder how they stood it. Stan called the engine room Dante's Inferno, and it actually seemed that way.

It was from the start a voyage of extremes: there had been long days of boredom when we had no sharks, and days when we had sharks but such awful weather we could not lower the cages. And a few days when everything went well and we could lower the cages into the feeding sharks. The *Terrier*'s gun had been removed before she left port, so we were following the whaling fleet, hoping their catch would attract, along with the other sharks a white shark for us to work with.

I constantly found myself struggling with my emotions. I saw great whales left to die, spouting blood from lungs that had been harpooned. I watched how the females, when their calves became exhausted during the chase, would not leave their young, but put themselves between the catcher and the calf. My friend Sam, who like all the crew had worked for the Japanese and Russians, said that the Japanese whalers would wound a calf, then shoot all the whales that tried to help. The pod doesn't leave a hurt juvenile, and it saved the bother of chasing them one at a time.

The following segment was recorded in my diary three weeks into the filming, and has been condensed for publication.

Saturday, April 26, 1969, A.M. We have just dropped off yesterday's whale completely unused at the flensing station, and are now looking for another. Unfortunately, the weather is still awful—overcast, squalls, and rough seas. Poor Peter Gimbel; he has so many problems without worrying about the weather.

Things improved rapidly during the day. The wind dropped away, the sun came out, and we found a whale with sharks. There was still a heavy swell running, but I prefer a swell to a short chop. I watched as the cages were lowered. There was less fuss than usual. The whale was bleeding well. How sad it looked in death! Another innocent victim of human greed.

The great white who starred in Jaws. *I always say there are sharks, and there is the great white. Certainly the fish stands alone at the pinnacle of nature's creations—huge, powerful, perfect. A great white is just that: a great white right from the day it is born. Anyone who has ever seen it alive and free in its natural element will never forget it.*

Peter Gimbel had worked out a plan of action for us divers. I was to try to swim among the sharks, while Stan, Ron, and Peter filmed, not only me but each other. Peter also wanted extreme close-ups of the sharks feeding.

We went down in the cages, leaving them dangling thirty feet below the carcass. The plan worked well until halfway to the whale. Suddenly, as if on call, the sharks lost interest in the whale on which they were feeding and became overwhelmingly attracted to us. We were completely surrounded by the gray marauders as they converged upon our tight little group, bumping and nuzzling.

From every direction they came. I was conscious only of myself, my companions, and the sharks. All else in the world was forgotten. I beat them off furiously with the powerhead, hitting the eyes and jabbing the gills with all my strength.

Peter, Stan, and Ron kept their cameras rolling. There was no need to look for action; it was everywhere. I thumped and whacked as fast as I could. Stan said afterwards he filmed a giant shark nuzzling my head. I remember feeling my hair being pulled and looking up to see an ugly snout and gaping jaw directly over my head. The sight gave me quite a shiver. I am glad someone filmed it.

Part of Peter's plan was to film, in close-up, sharks feeding on the whale, but we never made it. The sharks constantly beat us back. We ran out of film and air after what seemed a very short time and returned to the *Terrier VIII* for more of both.

I lay on the deck, the old timber planks soft and warm against my body, but within fifteen minutes we were all back with the sharks and into the action again.

This time, for some reason, the sharks were definitely less aggressive. I wanted to test my powerhead and tried my hardest, without success, to kill one. I had been given a different powerhead from what Ron and I normally use in Australia, and although I left an indentation on the shark's head, and once took a piece right out, the thing refused to detonate.

Via sign language, I was told all the things I was doing wrong, but was rather pleased when Peter Gimbel, trying the same stunt using my powerhead, met with similar success. (It was later discovered that the cartridge was wet, so I didn't feel too bad.)

Finally, between us all we must have hit the whole fifty or sixty sharks at least once, because one hard look, a shake of the fist, and they would shy away, rolling their eyes and jamming their gills tightly shut. Peter got all of the shots he had planned except close-ups of the sharks feeding. They did get some film of sharks swimming into the blood and hitting the whale, but clarity was poor and the action confused.

The magazine in Peter Gimbel's camera jammed for the umpteenth time. The poor guy. He was so upset by it, and I don't blame him. Jamming magazines are causing a lot of trouble. However, five rolls of good action came through okay.

We still have the whale, and all systems are go for a night dive.

Around 12:30 A.M., we finally left the bouncing Zodiac and entered the cages, which, to keep us close to the action, were tied to the whale. Peter Gimbel led the way, rolling camera-first

My dream shot of a great white shark. We had lowered the cage onto the sand when this shark swerved up over the bars. Fortunately, I was at that moment hanging out the window with my camera ready.

through the top hatch; then I followed. We had been diving constantly for days without a great deal of sustained action. The cool water was refreshing; it revived me, and I felt less tired. Peter was already waiting in the cage. The bubbles cleared, and I looked up towards the whale. It was my privilege to gaze upon a scene of life and death more horrible, more primeval, than any I had seen before. The whale's mutilated body streamed blood and guts into the current. Huge sharks, fifty...100...1,000—so many I couldn't count them—swirled in a frenzy around the carcass.

Where had they come from, these giant survivors from a bygone age? What ocean depths had hidden them from our view during the day, only to spew them forth in the darkness of night? I couldn't even guess. They swam with their mouths agape, some carrying great hunks of torn meat, gulping and swallowing without missing a beat of their powerful tails. The largest of them swam through the pack and hit the whale with tremendous force, shuddering his way into the torn belly until only his vibrating tail and anal fins protruded.

The lights, suspended some twenty feet beneath our cage, swung with the swell, casting an eerie glow into the green mist of blood. Sharks swept in and out of the light, graceful silhouettes adrift in an ocean of death. Then, flowing up from the darkness below, came a giant among giants: it was a tiger shark. Stretching somewhere from fifteen to eighteen feet, it dwarfed the oceanic whitetips. Peter and I watched awestricken as, with easy assurance, he took one of the swinging lights in his tremendous jaw, mouthing it over and over, plunging our primeval world into near darkness. Using the smaller hand light, we watched the massive shark with its night black eyes circle our cage several times before disappearing into the dark as though it had never been. Peter beat the bars with his fist. Like me he had thought for a minute that whitey (a white shark) had arrived.

Ron and Stan entered their cage, ghostly shadows in a web of silver steel. The heavy swell above was creating a pitching motion that quickly led to serious trouble. The ship's rise and fall did not match that of the whale to which our cages were attached, and because the power cable for our light was shorter than the rope tying our whale to the *Terrier*, the heavy light was almost impossible to hold. Eventually the strain on the power cable ripped it off our cage, all but dragging us out the open door. Stan and Ron were having even greater problems. Their light cable had immediately become entangled around the whale; from there it was twisted around our buoyancy tanks. They lost the whole lot after the first minute or so, but I was too busy hanging out the door trying to reach our own light cable as it swung past to be bothered with them. Peter was trying without much success to release their cable from our cage. It was a very unpleasant situation. Stewart Cody, the electrician, seeing our problem, leapt into the Zodiac, cut the cage free from the ship, and with exceptional skill and courage, started to untangle the twisted mess. The black ocean boiled with feeding sharks. They constantly bumped the rubber boat, making Stewart's job even more hazardous as he struggled with the heavy cables.

Beams of light from a distant sun ripple in brilliant waves across a great predator. The beast could have killed me in a moment, but we touched, and there came an understanding I could never fully explain. For a short time, I felt the shark to be my friend.

In the cage, we didn't realize our predicament. I wondered why we were unable to see the whale anymore, and why the light was failing, not realizing we were no longer tethered to anything, but adrift at night, surrounded by feeding sharks under the Indian Ocean.

Somehow Stewart sorted out the incredible muddle. We eventually got our light back again. Peter, with his usual great presence of mind, jammed the cable in the cage door. This gave me better freedom of movement, for the light was heavy and awkward, and I needed both hands to keep it under control. It was difficult to judge the direction Peter was shooting in, and even more difficult to maneuver the lights into the correct position. Mostly I judged my direction by watching the side of the camera housing and keeping the light coordinated with this. These lights don't seem as bright as the ones Ron uses and certainly are not as easily handled. They are more powerful, but the reflectors are not as efficient.

It was during one of our more difficult moments that a ten-foot oceanic shark chose to entangle itself in the harness on top of the cage. An exciting few moments followed, as we were buffeted madly from side to side. The shark finally thrashed its way free, and Peter gave me a look that said, "What next?" When "what next" eventually happened, it was something completely unpredictable. Somehow, both cages drifted into the whale. Ribbons of mutilated intestine streamed through the bars of our cage as they clanged together. The sharks had ripped open the whale's belly. Ron was wrestling to keep his cage free of the jawbone; although the cages were banging into each other, I could hardly see him for the blood and gore, which turned the sea into a sort of raw soup. I felt I was smelling, breathing, and tasting the stuff. I don't know how we left the whale; perhaps the Zodiac towed us away, but it was so pleasant to be free of that torn, smelling hulk that I almost felt happy. Peter showed me his gauge; it read zero. I still had 900 pounds, but that didn't help Peter. Stan, it seemed, was also breathing the ˙. Both he and Ron had run off a 400-foot roll of film. I released air into the buoy- ınd the cages surfaced. The Zodiac picked Ron and Stan up first. As they left the arks, as though on a signal, attacked the whale with renewed fury; our cage became ιary in a scene from hell.

y, without warning, a tremendous shock threw Peter against me, then we were d to the floor. The noise was almost unbearable; we had drifted into the ship's y were we bashed about by the steel cage, we were rising and falling in and out as the *Terrier* rolled side on to the swell. After what seemed like minutes, but was y seconds, we regained our feet. Peter handed out his camera and then, the per- an as always, came back down and made his "after you" sign. That was extreme- of him, because it meant he could give me a good push in the rear if I had trouble climbing onto the Zodiac. That night, however, he was pushing like mad, only I didn't want to go. More dangerous than any sharks, the *Terrier*'s massive hull rose and fell with terrifying power. The Zodiac was in an impossible position, and I hung on grimly until it repositioned itself, the cage grinding loudly into the ship's hull all the while.

Back on deck, an exhausted, trembling wreck, I heard how the cages had nearly been lost when cut adrift. We could not be seen in the dark; Stewart's quick thinking had saved us. He had the captain maneuver the *Terrier* downcurrent so he could pick us up as we drifted past; otherwise we would probably still be going. A postmortem the following day revealed that Ron's camera had jammed, an all-too-frequent happening, and that Stewart's hydrophone had been bitten off by a shark. All I can say is, better it than one of us. That night was the most dramatic experience ever.

Sunday, April 27, 1969. We had to tow our mutilated whale into the whaling station loading zone. We spent the day there, doing above water filming. It was not until our whale was pulled up that we could really appreciate the extent of the shark damage. Half of its body was completely eaten away. There were nine whales waiting to be processed. All were females, and all, quite probably, were pregnant. One somehow produced its fetus while lying on the loading ramp. A small, very beautiful female, perfectly formed—no wonder the whales were becoming scarce; they were not even given a chance to breed. What a curse the human race is—what sins did the innocent and peaceful commit to inherit the likes of us?

Monday, April 28, 1969. At sea, breakfast that morning was rather sparse. Apparently we were getting low on supplies; Kase, the Dutch cook, had not had a chance to restock for some time. Fortunately, it was a beautiful day. Catcher number twenty-five was chasing whales, and we were speeding toward it. Good weather waits for no one; there was only time for a few hours sleep before we were preparing to work under another whale.

By 8:30 the following morning, we were back in our cages. The sharks were still there, all of them, now joined by dozens of wandering albatrosses, whose round white chests and ungainly feet added comic relief to the circling crowd of sharks below. We left the cages, and again the sharks moved in to bump and jostle us, among them some immense blue sharks, who, with their slender bodies and big black eyes, are the most beautiful of all. Although I was bone tired, I jabbed and poked and pushed the sharks with all my strength, my arm beginning to ache from the constant jarring. The incredible intensity of the struggle had taken over my being; I could think of nothing but survival. My mind had regressed to another time, taking my body with it. I was a beast among beasts, for I had come to accept everything we were doing as normal.

Around 3:30 that afternoon, we made our last dive. I was on deck having a cup of coffee as the others prepared their equipment. Peter Gimbel never expected anyone to do what he wouldn't do first. (He was still after close-ups of shark's teeth tearing into the whale.) He said to me, "Valerie, I have to get these shots. It means leaving the cage and swimming to the whale. We could have trouble with the sharks so close to where they are feeding; there is no shame if you don't feel like coming."

My first thought was, we have successfully pushed our luck farther than we ever expected to, and now for the sake of a few close-ups, it's possible we will all die. I looked around the deck and felt the sun and the breeze and saw in fine detail the deckhands, my friends, and the rusting cabin of the *Terrier VIII*. I thought I might be looking at them all for the last time. Then I told Peter, "I'll follow you, but I want to see you out of the cage and up there first."

I was a little late entering the water. The men had been down about ten minutes. The scene around the whale was incredible. Our cages, as usual, hung thirty feet under the carcass, which had been reduced to no more than a heap of bloody flesh. Perhaps sensing that the end of their feast was coming soon, the sharks tore into the whale with renewed violence. Peter was swimming up through clouds of blood, protected by Stan, who was fighting a terrific battle with his exhausted powerhead. Further down, Ron was sitting atop the cage with his camera running. Dozens of huge, feeding sharks milled about, some hanging on the carcass, shuddering their way through the flesh, tearing, gulping, and swallowing in spasms of gluttony. I moved in to help Stan, my weariness vanishing as I whacked and thumped sharks as fast as I could. Peter, a hazy outline in the blood, was filming about four feet from the heads of a group of feeding sharks.

We formed a triangle with Peter facing the whale, calmly lining up his shots as though we were in an aquarium. Stan and I faced outward, hitting and hitting and hitting. A shark banged me so hard that I nearly dropped my stick. I looked down when another shark, about eight feet long, bumped me gently. I was amazed to see him actually mouthing my waist, and I felt a horrible tingle surging over my body. Then he pulled back, moving on instead to the whale. The gore clouding the water made it almost impossible to see. Suddenly, I found myself jammed against the bleeding carcass. An immense snout shoved in behind my back, pushing me aside as it went shuddering into the whale. For a moment I was immobilized, in a nightmare. The vibrating body sent a wave of weird shocks pulsing through me, then the blood cleared and I pulled away. The carnage surrounding us would have been no different a million years ago.

We had gone back in time, and we were caught in a struggle for survival where nothing from our world existed. I felt myself change. There was no fear, no pain, just a tremendous urge to survive. I was surrounded by the enemy and would fight to the end.

We would not learn of it until later, but below, Ron had been rammed so hard in the head by a huge shark that he had dropped his mouthpiece. Blackness came over him, and he nearly lost consciousness. Knowing no one could see him or save him, he rallied enough to crawl into the cage, until he recovered. Had he blacked out completely, he would have sunk into two miles of water without any of us seeing what happened. Even had we tried, there was so much blood pouring into the water, our vision was frequently limited to our immediate surroundings.

Peter finally gave his "film's out" sign, and we began our retreat, Ron swimming up to join us. As far as I could see, ominous shapes were gliding silently to and fro, sharks gorged to the hilt but reluctant to leave the banquet. We entered the cages and ascended; I felt like jelly, my arm aching from hitting sharks. Everything ached. Our trip back in time had ended.

All of us were tired, hungry, and cold, but hugely elated. Stan suggested that the sharks, realizing humans were not easy prey, had eventually decided to leave us alone, possibly because we seemed just another hungry species after a dead whale. Capping two days of fighting off sharks, this final dive had taken everything out of us. It was as if the four of us had gone into battle for nearly two days, and suddenly the battle had ended. We knew that no one else in the world had ever done what we had just done. We could now rest; it was an odd kind of satisfaction.

Ron and I couldn't eat, couldn't drink, couldn't even shower. We simply had to lie down. Eventually we tried some dinner, then crashed, exhausted, into bed again. But sleep eluded me. Whether my eyes were open or closed, all I could see in my mind were sharks, oceans of them. Swimming towards me, bumping me, nuzzling me; and I was fighting them off, wearily jabbing at them with my powerhead. At 9:30 I was still lying there in the dark fighting a thousand sharks, and Ron was tossing around too, as if he had a shark in bed with him.

"What are you doing?" I said. "Fighting sharks," he replied.

"So am I," I said. We both took tranquilizers and finally slept.

Perhaps the nearness of death becomes something too personal to talk about, for after that last dive, the four of us did not talk about our close calls. We were happy with each other, pleased with ourselves, for the film was in the can, but definitely not into enthusiastic conversation. We still haven't talked about it. I have never asked the others about it, and they have never asked me. To this very day, however, every moment of that dive under the whale is vivid, glued into my consciousness, there in my dreams.

The filming of *Blue Water White Death* would go on for another five months, four more of them on the *Terrier VIII* and one on a yacht called the *Saori*. The adventures were to continue as well, for we would dive from Durban to Mozambique to the Comoros, from Madagascar to the St. Lazarus Bank to Sri Lanka, from Astove to Europa to a dozen unnamed, unknown reefs.

We would finally take some superb footage of great whites off South Australia's Dangerous Reef. When this adventure eventually ended, *Blue Water White Death* had established Ron and me among the best-known divers in the world, and would lead Steven Spielberg to use us for the filming of *Jaws*. Other films would follow, among them *Jaws II, Gallipoli, The Year of Living Dangerously, Blue Lagoon, Orca,* and *The Island of Dr Moreau,* but each of these is another story in another time. The filming of *Blue Water White Death* stands alone in the annals of diving history. Nothing I did before and nothing I have done since can compare. It was and still is the pinnacle of my life.

Komodo

I remember Komodo.

To see something no one has ever seen, to experience something no one has ever experienced...that is the ultimate. I guess I'm very lucky; the pleasure of working with my underwater photographer husband and my love for the marine world have given me a lifetime of opportunities to explore new places and enjoy great adventure.

Few people ever have such a privilege, and even fewer, if the chance does present itself, have the courage to stop the life they're leading, even for a short time, and embrace the unknown. However, once you have taken that step, beyond the protection of your everyday life, you're doomed. Love of adventure is something that can never be sated. It may mean different things to different people, but the compulsion remains the same; no matter who you are or where you are, you'll go on reaching for more until the end of time.

In 1973 Ron and I first went to Komodo Island in Indonesia on board the cruise ship *Lindblad Explorer.* Lying 599 kilometers to the east of Bali, Komodo is high and barren. Its lofty peaks catch only infrequent rain-bearing clouds, except during the late summer monsoons, when the island briefly grows green and its few water courses run full.

Dramatic rather than beautiful, its steep slopes are sparsely dotted with tall lontar palms. In the lower valleys, some prickly brush manages to survive, but for most of the year, Komodo is a hot, dry, shadeless place where dragons hunt for deer and wild boar, and great whales swim in the bays. One small village of just 550 people manages to survive by fishing and collecting tamarind seed.

The dragons, which are really giant monitor lizards (*Varanus komodoensis*), are related to the common Australian goanna. They were first reported to the western world by an early aviator with engine trouble who landed on one of Komodo's beaches to carry out repairs. When the pilot, a Dutchman, brought back his stories of wild dragons fifteen feet long, they were treated more as a fabrication of his imagination than the truth. It wasn't until 1912, when Van Steyn, a Dutch military officer, brought two dead specimens back to the Zoological Gardens in Java, that the Komodo dragon was finally identified correctly.

Today, the great Komodo dragons still roam wild as they have for millions of years. The coming of man has made little difference to the dragons, for size and the ability to defend oneself are feared and respected by all living creatures. Komodo is a land and marine national park. Visitors wishing to see dragons no longer have to spend hours climbing the high mountains, harassed by heat, thirst, and exhaustion. It takes only an easy, two-kilometer walk inland to see enough big lizards to last a lifetime. As with most wild creatures, food is the catalyst. The sacrifice of a goat or two each month allows a regular population of dragons to exist in a small area easily reached from the shore. Yet, while it has become relatively simple to see the dragons, much of Komodo's underwater environment still remains a mystery.

In 1973, when I inquired about the possibility of diving and underwater photography around Komodo, I was told, "The diving isn't much, but the dragons are wonderful." They were right about the dragons, of course, but very wrong about the diving.

I remember taking off in an inflatable rubber Zodiac to check out the reef areas. It was just my husband, Ron, and me; everyone else had gone inland to see Komodo dragons. We anchored our Zodiac near a group of low rocks, 200 meters off a pink sand beach. Being an expedition ship, the *Lindblad Explorer* provided excellent diving and snorkeling equipment for the passengers, which was fortunate for us as the nearest diving facilities were hundreds of kilometers away. I suited up and, holding my camera, slipped off the pontoon into the hidden roots of Komodo. In a moment, I had left a hot and barren place of air and dust and was transported into a wet, cool world teeming with life. A thousand fish swarmed up to greet me...blue, yellow, pink, and silver. As we swam down the slope towards the reef, I saw orange gorgonian corals reaching to the surface, feather stars gracing every standing coral, starfish, anemones, urchins, crabs. The mixture was overwhelming in diversity, movement, and color.

I drifted, amazed. This was the true garden of Neptune, the center of all life. Animals lived on animals; space was in short supply. It was the most wonderful wild place I had ever seen and one of the most exciting.

Being the first anywhere is a thrilling experience, but the joy and wonder of Komodo's marine world was, and still is, beyond description. It was not simply a visual experience. Having evolved without an instinctive fear of man, after a few minutes most of the Komodo marine creatures, if approached in a gentle, unaggressive manner, tended to treat divers as just another marine animal. The Komodo fishes swarmed around us, not quite touching. Photography was difficult. The fish, full of curiosity, came too close. I could actually hear them swimming. Shrimps clicked, parrotfish munched the coral, the voices of three humpback whales filled the water, blending harmoniously with the smaller fish noises. It was a land of dreams, a place of magic. If mermaids lived anywhere, they had to live here.

The rocks glimmered before me, more colorful than a kaleidoscope. It was perhaps the most fragile collection of life on earth I'd ever seen, and certainly one of the most beautiful.

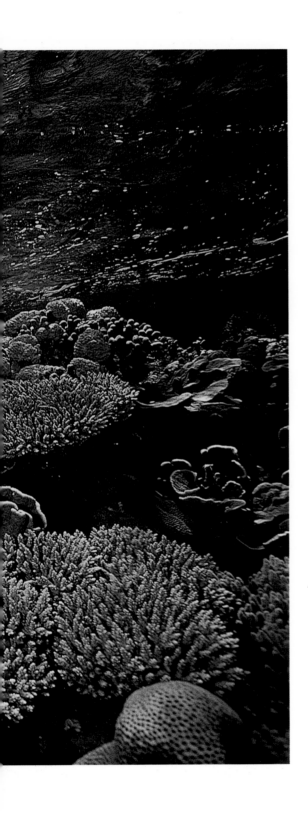

Rarely can such rich coral growth be found so close to the surface, for under normal circumstances, damage by sun and wave action in the shallows kills off most coral. Valerie's Rock on Komodo Island, Indonesia, with its calm surface and raging currents is the exception.

Like a great oak standing alone in a field, a soft coral towers above its platform of brain coral.

An astonishing variety of animals live inside one of the many caves that honeycomb the dropoffs around the Luci Para Islands, Indonesia. The long pink coral hanging from the roof is new to science.

Delicate clouds of translucent fish hung between the coral outcrops. Fusiliers shimmered past, a never-ending river of blue and gold. Nothing in my diving career had prepared me for such splendor. It was Nature's jewel box overflowing with living treasures.

I could scarcely move for wonder. I was seeing what no one had ever seen before, and it was a magnet that would draw me back again and again, for the rest of my life.

In September 1988, our friend and traveling companion, Australian Mike McDowell, organized a voyage of adventure and discovery on board an 111-year-old sailing vessel called the *Golden Hawk*. She is a very romantic-looking vessel, built of New Zealand Kauri. She is also not air-conditioned and very slow.

Indonesia is truly a country of extremes. Most people think of Indonesia as covered in rain forest or rice paddies. Few know of the dry places, desolate and unpopulated; even fewer would want to visit them. Our destination was the exposed off-shore rocks and islands on the southern side of Komodo Island. Lumps of sun-bleached earth and stone, they stand untouched as the great Sape Channel currents sweep around them; many are unnamed, many more uncharted.

Our first dive stop was locally called "Tikoh Gili Banta." It was a marvelous place for nudibranchs, feather stars, and sharks. I drifted, almost afraid of disturbing the perfection, a privileged visitor into the nation of fishes.

As is common around Komodo, living deepwater corals reached to the surface; the unusual was normal, the unexpected commonplace. The corals shimmered with orange anthias, jewel fish that rose and fell in gay clouds. White-tip reef sharks, the largest I had ever seen, moved through the fish; my presence concerned them not at all. Deeper down I could see gray reef sharks patrolling their territory.

I swam hopefully toward them, camera ready, but they appeared nervous and kept their distance. Suddenly, a moray eel rushed up toward me with what almost appeared to be a show of unexpected aggression. I pushed him off while swimming away up the slope, but the eel persisted,

and we both became quite frantic until I realized the creature didn't really want to tear out my jugular vein, but merely desired a piece of fish I had stuffed down my wet suit neck. (If possible, I always carry a piece of food to feed the fish while diving). It is rare for any eel to leave the safety of the reef, and as for following a large creature such as myself into mid-water, normally only eels who are long-standing friends behave that way. It seemed this eel was truly hungry, for he showed no fear and almost took my hand along with the fish when finally I gave it to him.

After such a display, I thought the eel, who was almost as long as myself, might pose for my camera. But he dashed back into a coral cave, where he cowered nervously, as though quite overcome by his recent uncharacteristic performance, and refused to emerge, no matter how I coaxed.

However, a few minutes later I was pleased that I had not wasted my film on a common moray eel, for a fat clown trigger appeared from behind a coral outcrop and swam toward me. In all my years of diving, I have rarely managed to get close enough to these beautiful fish for good photography, and here was one heading my way as though I were invisible. I checked my camera, held my breath, and waited.

The fish swam closer and closer. I was beside myself with excitement; then, the fish stopped five feet away and posed. I started taking pictures, speaking to the fish in my mind: "Move a little forward; face this way; stop by that coral." Sounds crazy, I know, but it is something I learned to do in the early days when I speared fish as a sport. I believe if I concentrate hard, I can actually will a fish into doing what I want. It may be my imagination, but it seems to work more often than not.

I was busy willing my clown trigger into even more attractive positions, when a sudden eruption of noisy bubbles had my subject dashing for cover and me swinging around in annoyance. Dennis, curious as to what I was doing, had swam over for a look, and not being a photographer himself, had little idea of the techniques needed to photograph a wild creature in its habitat.

He had brought a nudibranch to show me. Colored red, white, and black, the tiny shell-less mollusk was a species I had never seen before. Dennis's noisy arrival was immediately forgiven, and I carried my prize into shallow water where it crawled obligingly over a field of green algae while I photographed away. I could feel the water starting to move, but I was in the lee of a coral ledge and it didn't really bother me.

One of the reasons this area is so unexplored is the incredible tidal flows. They rush through the straits, swirling like rapids between the rocks and islands. Seven- or eight-knot currents are common. A diver in the water is completely at their mercy. Dhows, canoes, and even our sailing boat, the *Golden Hawk*, frequently make no headway at all against the flow.

It is both dangerous and deceptive. The water can be completely still and in sixty seconds become a rushing, uncontrollable, swirling mass. Whirlpools suck the surface into spinning funnels. Waves break against each other in total confusion, but most frightening of all is the strength of the flow. A diver has no more control of his or her body than a loose leaf has in the wind. There are few things that frighten me, but really strong currents are one of them.

Glowing like a rare jewel, the flesh of this coral polyp shines among its bed of brown. The colors that can make coral so vibrant are due to a small algae called zooxanthellae. This symbiotic algae lives in the tissue of the polyp. Without it, the coral would fade and die.

However, it is these same currents that are responsible for the amazing richness of marine life in this area. They continually pull nutrients from the deep channels, swirling them to the surface, and in so doing nourish the billions of static animals whose combined mass forms the living reef. This, in turn, creates a habitat for millions of small and medium-sized creatures attracted by this richness. Huge schools of fish, tuna, sharks, and rays fill the open water with shimmering movement. It is an exciting place to see and explore. For the inexperienced it can also be very dangerous.

By now my air was running low. The other divers were not in sight, but I could hear the pick-up dinghy's motor, so I headed toward the surface. As soon as I left the lee of the rock, the current carried me away, but I had expected this and surfaced waving to catch the attention

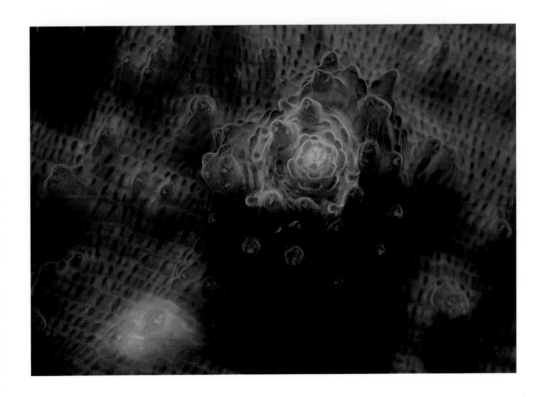

of our dive boat driver, who immediately came over. Everyone was out of the water except Ron, who appeared several minutes later, bobbing like a cork in the turbulence.

Life on the *Golden Hawk* was very simple. An Indonesian cook kept us supplied with as much rice, noodles, chili, and garlic as we needed. An Indonesian crew kept our scuba tanks, petrol tanks, and wine glasses full. They also sailed the vessel and drove our two wooden diving dinghies. It wasn't very fancy, but we really wanted for nothing; in fact, the *Golden Hawk*, for all her age, suited our needs very nicely.

Our next dive stop looked like an ideal location. The area was in a bay and protected from the tides. Unfortunately, probably because of this protection, the bottom down to about twelve meters had been dynamited into rubble. I complained to our boatman, and he laughed merrily. "Big boom, plenty fish," he said. "Many, many: all different."

"Don't the dynamite fishermen realize that they are destroying the future fishing in this area?" I asked.

"Oh yes," replied our driver, happily, "but no problem. Many more reefs, many more fish."

Dynamite fishing is against the law in Indonesia, but unfortunately, like many Indonesian laws, it is not enforced. In the last ten years, more and more once-rich marine areas have been blasted into lifeless rubble, and the government seems unwilling or unable to rectify the problem. Fortunately, some of the best areas are too deep for the dynamite fishermen to work successfully, but this does not preserve the future marine wealth that is easily accessible to tourists and fishermen alike. Deep water has its limitations where sightseeing is concerned.

As the days passed, we became more used to currents, swirling water, and patrolling sharks, until eventually it became normal to work out what could be safe places before a dive, so if anything went wrong, the divers would have a possible escape route already in their minds.

On the afternoon of September 11, we decided to dive the western side of a rock called "Nisa Leme." My first underwater impression was of spectacular scenery. The rock wall fell away sharply to one hundred feet, where a huge granite shaft rose in splendor, vertically, from the ocean floor. Some ancient movement of the earth's crust had split this monolith into two parts, creating a deep canyon.

Fascinated, I swam down into the shallow entrance. Gorgonian coral festooned the walls, and a thousand fishes faced the current. Then, with an unexpected suddenness, the current sucked me up. I grabbed for a coral but it pulled free, and I found myself dragged away, rolling over and over, ever more controlled by the water as it squeezed between the coral-covered walls of the split rock. There was little I could do but give myself up to the elements and enjoy the ride as best I could. Having just started the dive, there was no danger of running out of air.

Clutching my precious camera to my chest, I was suddenly thrown, at what seemed to me tremendous speed, straight into what looked like (and probably was) a dozen sharks and thousands of big fish. Startled by my sudden appearance and noisy bubbles, they scattered with much thumping of tails, leaving me breathless but unscathed.

I emptied my mask, which had partially flooded, and checked instantly for any danger. My depth gauge read 100 feet. Not wanting to drift away, I hung onto a blue-edged table coral flapping like a flag in the current until I managed to wedge my leg under a rock and hold myself steady.

Corals are a good standby subject when nothing else is happening. I love the challenge of making dull subject matter look dramatic and there-fore interesting. Usually, I rely on composition more than any other single thing. Good composition pleases the eye, and that's what photography is mostly about, visual pleasure.

The sharks were gone, but the fishes stayed, circling me with what must have been utter amazement. I photographed away until lack of both air and film forced me up the slope to the surface. I swam up, slowly decompressing as I went. Being stricken with that dreadful diver's malady, the bends, in such an isolated place would not only be very careless of me, but because of our isolation, possibly fatal.

Back on the *Golden Hawk* everyone had a story to tell. Mike and Mark had been diving the western side of the island. "It's much better around there," said Mark, "but you have to keep behind rocks or you get carried away. Even the sharks sit in the lee of the rocks; it's incredible, you swim from rock to rock, hanging onto the bottom to pull yourself along." This I had to see. Sharks sheltering in the lee of rocks really did sound incredible.

It took an hour to refill our tanks. Then we were off again to Nisa Leme. The western side was more rugged. Rocks and ridges shone softly beneath the surface; beyond that was noth-ing, just the blue-black depths.

I slipped in. It was awesome scenery—not scary, just awesome. Like the Grand Canyon or the surface of the moon. Black surgeon fish schooled by the thousands, blocking the sunlight as they passed. Tuna patrolled the deeper edges, and there seemed to be sharks everywhere: small reef whitetips around the coral and gray reef sharks fur-ther down. What wasn't there were the sharks hiding behind rocks. Then I realized the current had ceased, and they were probably all swimming in the open while they had the chance.

It was one of the best diving and pho-tography locations I had ever seen. The small fish life was incredible, and the diver-sity of species beyond anything we had so far witnessed. Certainly I needed more than one camera, so I surfaced and yelled for the boatman to bring my Nikonos with the 20mm lens. He came immediately, the sharp blue bow heading straight for my waving arm, but when he reached me the silly man did not cut the engine, just ran forward with the camera while I struggled with one hand to hold onto the gunnel.

Unfortunately as I reached up for my camera, a loop of trailing rope tangled around the valve on my dive tank, and I found myself being towed along backwards with a camera in each hand and an inexperienced Indonesian boatman who insisted on trying to free me while the motor kept chugging away. The greater my fury, the more desperate became his useless efforts. We had no common language. My greatest terror was that I would drop a camera in deep water; my second worry was the propeller whizzing around somewhere close to my legs, for I seemed to be traveling along face up and could only see sky, the side of the dory, and the terrified-looking boatman who had replaced our usual assistant for the afternoon.

To make matters worse, he had a cigarette in his mouth and the ash kept falling into my face. Finally, almost exploding with rage, I just screamed "Stop, stop, stop, or I'll kill you." Obviously, he had heard these words before, because it had the desired effect; he stopped the motor, and once the pressure lessened, I actually fell free.

Now I was in deeper water and some distance from the rock, but not wishing to trust myself to the boatman again, I decided to swim back. The boatman, obviously relieved to be free of me, motored away, and I felt rather lonely in all that water with only a barren rock as a guide. Eventually, I saw the jagged, coral-encrusted boulders rising below me and, with not a little relief, swam down. The water became colder as I neared the bottom, and the coral growths larger and less diverse. I could see the tail of a shark protruding from a cave.

Akira was diving close by, so I gave my high-pitched yelp which carries well underwater, and means "come here." Used to my yelps, Akira swam across instantly, and as he focused his camera, I gave the shark's tail a mighty tug.

The imaginative use of lighting can make even a simple subject such as this leather coral, left, an attractive photographic subject.

A pink brittle star hides from potential predators on pink soft coral. This type of camouflage is common throughout the marine world. It always makes me wonder how the starfish knows it is the same color as the soft coral, for I have seen identical creatures yellow in color on a yellow coral.

Luckily the creature lurched forward, giving me time to raise my camera also, then it spun around and swam straight under me. I had expected to see the tropical tasseled wobbegong (*Orectolobus ogilby*), but to my absolute amazement, it was the colder water species *ornatus* who went dashing away. I had noticed quite a few species of temperate zone fishes swimming in the cool upwellings but had never thought to see this sluggish, bottom-dwelling species so far north. Although commonly found around southern Australia, and well up the New South Wales coast, *ornatus* is usually replaced by the smaller tasseled wobbegong in tropical waters.

A week later, on board the cruise ship *Island Explorer*, we were joined by Dr. Jack Randall from the Bishop Museum in Honolulu, who explained that throughout the world there were cold areas both above and below water that became isolated by the warmer climate as the last Ice Age diminished. Most subtropical flora and fauna receded toward the poles, maintaining pace with the cooler temperatures. But the few species that remained, trapped by evolution and an unchanging climate outside their normal range, are of tremendous scientific value.

The last Ice Age existed around 9,000 years ago. Plants and animals of the same species, separated by vast climatic barriers, had continued to evolve as their distant counterparts did. It seems scientists studying living specimens from these temperate zone time capsules can better determine the process of evolution.

Perhaps the most amazing aspect of evolutionary research is its demonstration of how little life changes, even over millions of years, when left in a suitable, stable habitat. Jack, when he saw Ron's video of the fish, became very interested. He was rather surprised about the *ornatus*, though, and looked a bit doubtful until I told him I had photographed it and would send him a copy.

Two days later, I had an experience that made being towed backwards by my dive tank seem almost pleasant. We anchored the *Golden Hawk* off Lankoi Rock, south of Lankoi Island, and lowered the dinghies. The water, as usual, was boiling around the island and rushing like rapids past the rock. This sinister-looking place was Mike's choice. Even above water it looked unpleasant. The current humped over the rock like a fat waterfall to swirl away in a nasty looking whirlpool.

"It doesn't look very inviting," I remarked to Ron, who answered, quite logically, "All of these places have a lee; just stay on the downcurrent side of the rock, and you should be all right." Thinking back, a smart person might have taken more notice of the "should" in Ron's answer. The lee was right under the whirlpool.

I rolled over the gunnel and swam like mad for the promised lee. Akira and Michiko followed us, racing towards the hoped-for protection of Lankoi Rock.

From the beginning, it was not a fun place to be. Several pinnacles of granite rose vertically from very deep water. The static marine life was colorful but stunted. No less than a million sea urchins lived on the inhospitable walls, and fire corals predominated.

Almost immediately, everyone seemed to be having trouble; in fact, we were all bunched together in the dubious lee on the rock's southern side, desperately trying to hang on without being perforated by a bunch of sea urchin spines.

There were plenty of large fish and sharks swimming past, none of which interested me very much as I could not move away from the rock toward them. It was difficult diving, but I could see some strange ascidians below me and dragged myself down thirty meters to photograph them. After perhaps twenty-five minutes, I noticed I was alone, and as my air was running low, I decided to begin ascending, planning a decompression stop in a crack I had noticed about three meters from the surface.

By now, the current seemed even more ferocious, and I clawed my way up the rock face. The water swirled around me like a liquid hurricane. Then, to my horror, about nine feet from the surface, I was plucked from the rock face and carried away, bubbles and all, out and down, frantically clearing my ears as I went.

The rock disappeared from view. I felt helpless. I was helpless. It got darker, colder; my flippers seemed to have lost their power. I checked my depth: forty meters; air: 500 pounds. Not

Jellyfish are related to corals. They start life as tiny planktonic medusas floating helplessly with the ocean currents. Unlike the juvenile corals seeking a permanent home, this jellyfish can never settle and must spend its life drifting, a glutinous speck of life in a vast ocean.

many breaths left at 120 feet. Suddenly I saw the bottom of a dark-encrusted rock. I remember thinking, "I am going to be crushed; flung into the bottom and held there." But one meter from what appeared to be total disaster, I was jettisoned sideways and up. The base of the rock went flying past, and I scrabbled at growths, striving for control, desperate to free myself from the whirlpool. But my handholds tore away, and I swirled on, accompanied by the rubble and weed I had clutched at in passing.

The surface appeared, and I thought, "Valerie, you have to swim harder than ever before; you have to make the surface." As the flow began taking me away once more, I swam my hardest for the surface, my toes bunched up inside my flippers lest flying water rip them off.

I broke the surface and screamed. Two opposing currents seemed to be crashing into each other. The water boiled, and my kicking legs were being pushed around like a rag doll's.

But they had heard my scream in the dinghy, and just when I felt my strength would last no longer, I saw the blue hull bouncing toward me and knew I was saved.

My companions had abandoned the dive early and were watching for me to surface. Fortunately, they were not far away, but because of the turbulence, they had to approach with caution. Afterwards I was so exhausted I could barely climb back on board the *Golden Hawk*. It had definitely not been one of my more enjoyable dives, and Lankoi Rock was wiped forever from my list of good places to go.

Perhaps the most amazing aspect of my uncontrolled ride was the huge numbers of school fish and sharks I passed, all of whom swam around quite naturally as though the water were almost still. We humans are certainly not built for an aquatic life!

The *Golden Hawk* left us at the isolated bay where we had first discovered Komodo's secret beauty so long ago. It was here that we were to join a lovely Indonesian vessel called the *Island Explorer* and travel to the wonderful Banda Sea, an area we know well and visit often.

As was fitting, I had my last Komodo dive at that place where it all began sixteen years before, off the pink sand beach, where the dragon tracks lead down to the water and whales sing in the bay. The yellow and blue sweetlips still hung shyly behind a curtain of fry, and our old friend the crocodilefish lay in a bed of living flowers, trying his best to look like a colony of polyps. Fish clouded the water with their brilliance; the living beauty of the static reef animals was beyond description, or comparison. The place moved, it sang, it was dynamic; it was also tranquil.

It was the marvelous marine world of Komodo Island.

Beyond the reach of conscious thought is a world populated by creatures whose lives are as mysterious to us as the outer planets. They live, love, and die, their ways known only to themselves. Such is their habitat. We humans can visit but briefly, our eyes seeing the myriad life forms as a mass of color and shape.

Some animals have evolved to live both in the ocean and on the land. For them, the marine world holds no mystery; it is as familiar as the dry shoreline on which they sleep. The most endearing of these is the sea lion. Sea lions are nature's fringe dwellers, moving from one world to the other with familiar ease. They enjoy the best of both worlds, which is perhaps why they seem to possess such happy natures.

The Australian Sea Lion

E ared seals (*Neophoca cinerea*), or, as most Australians call them, sea lions, must be about the cutest, sweetest, and most lovable of all sea creatures. They look delightful, and they are.

All animals appeal to me in varying degrees, but sea lions I love, and I've loved them from the very first time I saw them.

Australian sea lions are amongst the rarest sea creatures in the world. They exist in family groups on small islands and reefs off the southern Australian coast. Humans are one of their enemies; another is that living eating machine, the great white shark. But whereas the white shark normally attacks only sick, old, or very slow sea lions, humans, in their usual fashion, are generally not so discriminating.

On January 15, 1973, the sea lions on Dangerous Reef numbered between twenty and forty animals. Five years before at the same time of year there had been hundreds; I know because I tried counting them myself and reached over 200 before I stopped.

At the time we were working from the *Temptation*, a Kangaroo Island fishing boat skippered by Bill Zealand. We anchored 200 yards from the main island in the Dangerous Reef formation, and all went ashore to film an above-water segment on sea lions for our television series *Taylors' Innerspace*. This episode, called "Maneater," required several sequences showing interaction between family groups, and how in play, pups become careless. It was during this shoot that I realized how depleted the number of sea lions on the main reef had become, and also how unusually afraid the remaining animals were.

Where had all the sea lions gone? Perhaps they had moved on. They also could have died of natural causes; however, I think in the name of sport, some may have become shark bait, and many more had suffocated, tangled in fishermen's nets. Others had possibly left for safer reefs further away from Port Lincoln and its human-oriented dangers. In the early seventies, sea lions and dolphins were still being used to attract sharks to some game boats. With the proper introduction of protection laws, this cruel practice has happily ceased and today their numbers have increased dramatically.

I am writing this story hoping that other people may begin to understand how wonderful a wild, unhunted creature can be. It would indeed be a good thing if everyone could know the Australian sea lions as I do. In their presence the world seems full of joy and innocence; they are a delight to behold, and they give friendship without question.

We finished filming around Dangerous Reef and moved to an isolated island further south, looking for sea lions in larger numbers. Although we had shot several scenes on the Dangerous Reef sea lions, compared with what we knew could be obtained using animals who were not so afraid of us, it was fairly poor quality.

Our skipper, Bill Zealand, anchored his boat just out from a sunny, sheltered cove on Hopkins Island, west of Dangerous Reef. Ron and I donned our wet suits and loaded our underwater cameras. For us it was a fun dive, particularly after our white shark filming of the previous few weeks. Being banged about in a little metal cage with the big sharks munching around may be very exciting, but is hardly good fun if you have to do it day after day in a big swell.

A few years ago I was sitting on Dangerous Reef, South Australia, waiting for Ron, who was off filming cormorants. It was a hot, sunny day, and I guess I was dozing a little when I felt something soft pushing against me. A pup about six weeks old had cuddled up on my shady side. I was ecstatic; I wanted Ron to see me, but I didn't dare move in case I frightened the little fellow. I sat still as a stone, while my left hand slowly moved up under the pup's neck and began to gently stroke him. He rolled against me, one soft little webbed-fingered flipper resting on my thigh. I was in heaven. The pup, having no instinctive fear of man, treated me much as he would another young sea lion, with total trust. I wanted to hug and kiss him but knew such human acts of emotion would break the spell. It was a privileged moment, simple, unplanned, unforgettable. If only every human could have such an experience, what a difference it would make to the world, and those we share it with.

On the tiny beach, a group of about seventy eared seals could be seen. Two young males were having a practice fight watched by their big daddy, who also watched us; the rest dozed peacefully. Ron and I slipped into the water and swam quietly toward shore, a distance of about 300 meters.

Several sea lions appeared interested, but showed no real alarm until we started to crawl from the water and up the beach. The effect of our unexpected appearance was overwhelming to say the least; the big brown bull bellowed a warning, and seventy sea lions galloped down the beach toward us. It was rather a nerve-wracking sight, even though I knew they meant no harm.

Running down the flat, sandy beach they hit the water much faster than we had anticipated. There was tremendous splashing and roaring all around us, then silence; we turned and looked seaward into seventy pairs of gentle brown eyes. It was all so unexpected—panicked flight had become incredulous curiosity. They sat in the water, muttering to each other, and although I couldn't understand the language, my ears burned a bit.

Ron, like me, has a great affection for our sea lions and loves to play with them. To see what would happen, Ron jumped up; so did all the sea lions. I jumped up; seventy sea lions jumped too. It was like magic. We ducked under and looked around—seventy sweet faces looked around also. It was truly a delightful moment. It was too shallow near the beach for good filming; all this jumping up and down had created an underwater sandstorm, so surrounded by our furry retinue, we swam into deeper water.

Used to the less friendly Dangerous Reef sea lions, I was nervous at first, for they came so close, so fast, that collision seemed inevitable. But it was only a game. I started to enjoy myself and take photographs. Ron's movie camera could be heard whirring away as the streamlined actors performed for him. I began to notice the sea lions' more interesting habits—there were no pups, only chubby little yearlings who still stayed close to their mothers. A female would often take a pup between her front flippers and give it an underwater cuddle. Even the big old bull seemed affectionate toward his offspring and would sometimes give one a big hug to his chest. They would also put their arms around each other in a very fond fashion. In fact, they seemed one of the happiest and most loving family groups I had seen for a long time.

One problem that I couldn't solve easily was keeping them away from the camera. There always seemed to be one, often two sea lions peering down the lens, and the more I moved back, the more they followed.

At one stage I was swimming along when suddenly one of my legs wouldn't move. Startled, I sprang around, only to find a cheeky sea lion holding my flipper in her mouth.

I shook my fist, she shook her flipper, so I did the only thing possible—I sat on the bottom with a seal on my flipper and waited for her to tire of the game, which, now that I was motionless, happened almost immediately. The only problem was that every time I tried to move, a sea lion would once again grab my fin. Ron had one nibble his hand very gently, though she certainly had the teeth to take his hand off had she wanted to, but it was just friendly curiosity. I gave the still camera to Ron, and he took a shot of me with a sea lion. We just sort of looked at each other, nose to nose.

After our experience with the white shark in the same area several years before, I felt a little wary for a while. The shark had appeared at great speed; the sea lions had vanished, leaving Ron, me, and Italian film producer Bruno Vailati to handle the problem. We hid in the weeds while the shark circled. Eventually it decided we were not what it was after and disappeared. This time there was no shark problem, and up until now, though we have been back many times, no white sharks have appeared.

Some females have excellent taste in men; one plump lovely became enraptured with Ron. Right from the beginning she stood out as being extra friendly. She examined Ron's flippers, then his head. Ron, who by this time was well up on sea lion etiquette, offered his hand to be kissed (a sign of true friendship among sea lions). She kissed his hand, then the top of his head, then his ear and his faceplate. Ron ended up sitting on the bottom among the weeds, a blonde lovely in his arms. Rodney Fox, who was with us at the time, also received similar attentions from this outrageous flirt. I was ignored. As is often the way, both men lost interest in me and concentrated on their new star. Unwanted, I drifted away by myself to take stills of a sad-eyed young bull, who didn't seem interested in me either

Young sea lion pups appear to pair off much the same as young children. They seem to have a chosen companion, both in and out of the water, someone special to play with. A most touching example of this friendship happened near Pearson Island, forty miles out from Elliston, South Australia. Ron, I, and (at the time) abalone fisherman Rodney Fox were diving among huge boulders in fifty feet of water. Ron was filming Rodney collecting abalone when three half-grown young pups joined us. They belonged to a colony that lived on the island about a mile away from where we were anchored. It seemed they were out for a day of fun and adventure. They were an absolute delight; two of them played around us for almost an hour, chewing Rod's airhose and Ron's flippers. One, however, hung back, never coming very close. His friends would play with us for a minute or two, then one would return to his reluctant companion, put his arm around him and try to bring him over. This happened a dozen times or more; the shy little sea lion would let his friend bring him to within twenty feet, then, apparently overcome by fear, would dart away. We could see what looked like nylon shark net around his neck. It was touching the way his friends cared for him; they seemed to know he wasn't completely well.

Back on board Rodney's twenty-foot fiberglass boat, I could see the three sea lions playing in the water; one appeared slower than the rest. I asked Ron if we could try and capture him to remove the net; both Ron and Rodney seemed to think the idea pretty impossible, but felt we should try. It was my job to work out how we should go about trapping him. The following day I presented my plan. It was very simple: we would sneak up on the sea lions while they were having a nap (sea lions love to nap), and throw a net over the young pup. Although it seemed doubtful that we could achieve this without stirring up the whole colony and causing mass panic, we decided to try. First we drove by the colony in our boat to check out the terrain. It was a warm day, and nearly all the sea lions were asleep. Our quarry was lying next to his mother, fortunately near the edge of the group. Had he been in the center, creeping up on him would have been impossible. They hardly gave us a second glance as we cruised past; we landed on a small sandy beach nearly sinking our tiny dinghy in the surf. On shore Ron prepared a large net by wiring an old sack onto the boat hook handle. It looked a bit clumsy, but under the circumstances it was the best we could do.

Pearson Island consists of what must be one of the world's most incredible rock formations; it's virtually a giant rockery towering above the southern ocean. Rodney said "God took a little bit of all that is wonderful and when he put it together, it became Pearson Island." The main body of sea lions were sleeping on a

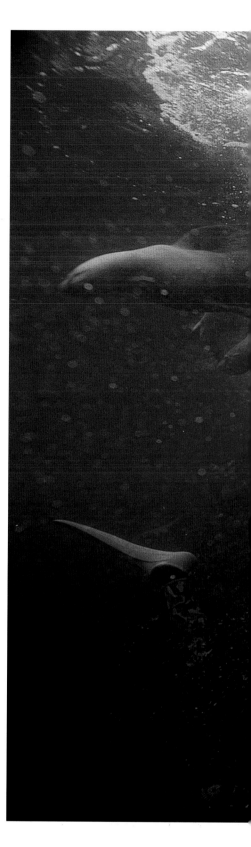

Ron has an amazing ability when it comes to directing marine creatures. Just what he wants this sea lion to do is not clear, but he is certainly getting an interesting reaction. The sea lions seems to love Ron. They follow him around, their curiosity never satisfied. Ron says they hear his camera and want to see where the noise comes from. I think it's because they know he loves them, can move like they do, and is always gentle.

smooth granite slope about half a mile west of the beach; it was rather a rugged climb to reach the slope. Rodney carried the movie camera, Ron his net, and I carried the still camera, a second net, scissors, and a knife. Unfortunately, once we reached the granite slope, the boulder piles finished, and there was no cover. We kept low and made no sound, moving towards the sea lions in quick bursts. To a sea lion, standing erect is considered a position of attack; by keeping crouched down, we remained on a level of friendship and were less likely to draw attention to ourselves. Several sea lions were awake; we took even greater care not to be noticed by them, spending minutes crouched motionless when a sea lion looked in our direction. About forty feet from the sea lions we waited for our chance; when, after several minutes, it came, Ron ran first, with me pounding along behind. The whole colony leapt up, roaring with fright, and galloped down the slope. Our quarry's mother called her baby, but too late; as the little fellow jumped up, he jumped right into Ron's sack. We both leapt on him; his mama cried her alarm as she ran into the sea, looking back as she did so.

The pup lay still; already blood from his neck was staining the sack. I gave Ron the scissors. He hacked a hole in the sack behind the seal's head, exposing a tangle of 100-pound monofilament line. The scissors sawed their way through the tough nylon; they were only nail scissors so it was hard work, but the knife was useless. The pup whimpered in pain as Ron pulled each piece of line up; there was so much of it. I could feel the soft furry body wincing with every tug. It took ages, but eventually his head and ears were free. We rolled him on his back; quickly Ron hacked another hole through the bloodstained sack. How had the pup survived so long? Shark meshing had been stopped in South Australia six months previously; the line must have been tangled around him for at least that long.

The terrible wounds at his throat oozed pus and blood all over us. Ron gouged into the smelly mess with scissors, pulling out strand after strand of knotted nylon line. I was nearly sick with horror; in places his flesh had grown around the line, and removing these pieces must have hurt cruelly, for he whimpered sadly. Ron's scissors were digging over an inch into the soft flesh. Poor little soul; he had been suffering a long time. His mama watched worriedly from the water's edge, calling out every now and then. It was sickening. It seemed the amount of shark line was endless, but we couldn't leave a single strand—it would strangle him just as surely as 100 strands. We did leave several short pieces under the flesh near his little ears; they were knotted, and to pull them through could damage his ears beyond repair. Nature would have to take care of those; we had done our best. Ron cut the sack completely open, and the fat baby rolled out. Mama bellowed and he ran down to her, diving into the water. As we watched, he turned to look at us, then dived again, shaking his head in disbelief as he did so. All the family came and gathered at the water's edge, looking up at us. I wondered what they were thinking; certainly we had not made them afraid. What a pity we were leaving the following day; it would have been interesting to study the reactions of the little sea lion next time he met us underwater.

Another astounding incident that took place during our South Australian shoot happened while we were filming sharks. A thirteen-foot great white had just swum up the oil slick and was circling the *Temptation*. To let him know he had found the right place, we threw out some baits, which, after some hesitation, he took. We were suiting up to enter the cages, when a young bull sea lion arrived. There were seven of us on board; we all stared in amazement, for the sea lion followed the shark's tail around and around, darting up to his head and then darting away. It gave every indication that it was chasing the shark, sometimes leaping from the water for an extra quick rush. It was obvious the shark felt agitated; he swam faster. The sea lion pestered him all the more. Finally the shark swam away. I could hardly believe my eyes: a sea lion had chased away our shark. It had taken us several days and a hundred pounds of chum to entice the white shark in; now we would have to start again.

The young bull swam calmly back to his family on nearby Dangerous Reef, where he promptly flopped down on a sunny rock and went to sleep. Apparently chasing sharks was all in a day's work for him.

At the time of writing, in all of Australia there are between 9,300 and 11,700 Australian sea lions. Out from Port Lincoln where these stories took place, almost 6,000 sea lions live. In the 1960s, when we first visited the sea lions, there appeared to be twice that number. At that time they were not protected. Eared seals are now completely protected in Australia. Sadly, they're still dying. Professional fisherman with their nets take an enormous toll in what is called accidental bycatch. This unfortunate situation will only change when net fishing is no longer viable.

Ron and I believe the Australian sea lions to be the most intelligent of marine animals. They are unique to South and Western Australia, living in colonies on offshore reefs and islands. They are our favorite of all marine animals. I shall visit, observe, and photograph these animals whenever I can. I love them totally and think of them often. Just knowing that they exist and are accessible has enriched my life greatly. When all else fails, there will always be the sea lions, ready to share their lives and give their friendship.

It's a lovely thought, isn't it?

The Filming Of Jaws

After filming *Blue Water White Death*, we worked on the underwater segments of a thirty-nine-part television series called *Barrier Reef*, unaware that sharks would soon loom ever larger in our future. Several other films followed, then in 1973 we received the galley proofs of a book written by an as-then-relatively-unknown writer named Peter Benchley. Hollywood producers Richard Zanuck and David Brown wanted to know what we thought of the story and if it would be possible to film a great white shark behaving in a fashion similar to the shark in Peter Benchley's book. We felt it could be done, but a great deal of time would be needed to coax the shark into performing like the thinking, vindictive beast in Peter's story.

Universal wanted the live shark footage quickly to allow them to organize the above water action so it would intercut smoothly. To help with the more complicated scenes, it was decided to make an eight-meter mechanical shark, essential for scenes showing actors and shark together. Ron flew to Los Angeles to help with the design of the mechanical shark. The end result was actually three mechanical sharks, one that moved left to right, a right-to-left model, and a front-on model. Hydraulic cables from the surface controlled each movement of these man-made monsters, which meant that every time the entire great white appeared on the screen, it had to be a real live animal. The model sharks were so realistic that despite abundant publicity about the mechanical sharks, many people continue to believe sharks really behave like the fish in *Jaws*. The footage was so convincing.

On February 16, 1973, we set out from Port Lincoln on the thirty-five-foot *Trade Wind*, skippered by Dick Leech. Dick is cheerful, hard-talking, and a fine seaman. To make our fourteen-foot sharks appear twenty-four to twenty-six feet long, we had everything half-size: cages, tanks, a stunt diver, even a second boat, Rod Fox's eighteen-foot fiberglass *Skippy*, which was about half the size of Quint's fishing boat in the book. Production Manager Jim Hogan also brought Carl Rizzo, a former jockey who had doubled for children on horseback in feature films. Although Carl's diving experience consisted of only a couple of brief scuba lessons in a pool, Hollywood assumed that we would be able to bundle this shy, quiet little man into a cage, tie baits to the bars, lower him and the cage into the icy, turbulent southern ocean, and wait for the sharks to attack. I guess that is the sort of stuff Hollywood lives on, but to those of us who knew sharks and the ocean well, it all seemed incredible.

On the way to Dangerous Reef, a brisk southeasterly whipped the southern ocean into a living carpet of white and blue. We anchored the *Trade Wind*, lowered chum buckets, and strung shark baits along the hull. The sloppy swell created an uncomfortable anchorage, but we had no choice and settled down to wait. On the reef itself were hundreds of Australian sea

The great white takes a salmon from the tease rope. There is no hook in the bait; it is merely a means of keeping the shark swimming around the cages searching for more handouts. Scenes like this are becoming harder to photograph due to the decrease in the population caused by fishermen.

lions, many with newly born dark brown babies. Sea lion pups are not born swimmers, and during their learn-to-swim period, many fall victim to nature's culler, the great white shark.

Three days later our first shark moved up the chum slick. The cage was rolled over the stern, and Ron climbed down onto the duckboard. The shark was a good one, thirteen feet long, and he came straight in to feed. Ron shot four hundred feet of film, then changed cameras. The first scenes of *Jaws* were in the can. We didn't know it, but audiences the world over would never think about sharks in the same way again.

With two possible feature films in mind, Universal wanted Ron to shoot enough footage of white sharks during this expedition to cover extra scenes they might need in the future. It was interesting that we had no proper script. Normally, a cameraman likes to have the script requirements laid out to provide a mental image of the needed scenes and how they should be shot. With *Jaws* it worked in reverse. Except for a few key shots, the underwater sections of the script would be written around the behavior of live sharks in the wild. Clever movie-making that was to lend tremendous authenticity when footage of the mechanical sharks was cut in.

After lunch I made a dive dressed like the scientist in the film, and Ron shot a roll of over-the-shoulder takes of my hands on the cage bars and of me reaching out to touch the shark as it passed. The rough surface conditions tossed the cage around, making steady photography impossible. Around mid-afternoon the shark apparently became bored with us and left.

The following day a steady drizzle fell. To everyone's great joy, a new shark arrived, and we began to tease him with the baits. Ron immediately climbed into the cage. The *Trade Wind* pitched like a mad thing, and the wind blew like ice from the South Pole. My nose told me that in spite of the cold, the baits were beginning to ripen rather well. Only the shark seemed unaffected by the weather and the rolling boat. Ron decided he wanted Carl down in his smaller cage, which for purposes of the film was attached to the abalone winch on Rod's boat. "We shouldn't waste a good shark," he said, and Jim agreed. Carl didn't seem happy, but we suited him up and he crossed to Rod's boat. A more reluctant diver would be hard to imagine.

Dick and Rod lowered Carl into his small cage, but no sooner had he disappeared under the surface than they had to pull him back up; water had entered his mouthpiece. Three times Carl tried to go down in his cage, but without success. He was too inexperienced to handle the rough seas. Finally Ron was forced to abandon the idea and wait for calmer conditions. It was a great pity, for the shark was an excellent performer, bashing into the cages again and again. I suspect that this wild shark action had something to do with Carl's reluctance to dive. It can be scary enough for a diver with experience. For a diver without it, it must have been horrendous.

We had to wait almost a week for the weather to improve. It was still not calm, but at least it was sunny. All morning we watched, but no sharks came. I made lunch, and while the men were eating, I wandered out on deck and started throwing minced tuna into the water. After about ten minutes a thirteen-foot shark appeared and started cutting to and fro through the fish particles. I called "Shark," and threw some blood in his path. Lunch forgotten, everyone immediately leapt into action. Here is what I wrote in my diary at the time.

26-2-74: Dangerous Reef, South Australia...

The big shark liked blood. He moved closer. Tasting the water. More minced tuna was thrown in and Ron's cage lowered. Carl's smaller but much heavier and stronger cage was manhandled into position next to Rodney's boat and held in place by a hand-operated abalone winch. Carl was suited up and helped into his cage. Conditions were calmer now than they had been in weeks. From the deck we could see the brute circling around. It is terribly frustrating to be down in the cage, watching and waiting, every nerve concentrating on the shark, wondering from which direction he will emerge. On deck we could see the shark before Ron. I tried to will the shark closer to the cages. I think we all did, but the beast paid no heed to our silent thoughts and kept his distance.

Frustrated, Ron surfaced and climbed back on board. Carl was also brought to the surface; he had managed very well; only the shark had performed poorly. Ron and Carl had been on deck a few minutes when a new shark appeared. He came straight and strong, fearing nothing, a shark that moved, thought, and behaved like the fish Peter Benchley had written about so convincingly in his book.

I loaded a 303 bullet into the powerhead on my speargun and placed it within easy reach. Then I told Greg Dean, the assistant, that if there was any trouble, I would jump in the water with the gun, and that I expected him to help me in the water. Greg said, "Sure" and he meant it too. Immediately, Ron put on a fresh scuba tank, asking Carl to do the same. The shark circled closer, Ron's cage bouncing as the fish attacked the flotation tanks. We could all see Ron, six feet down, sitting on top of his cage filming, a rather risky method he had been using for some time to get shots without bars in the foreground. Not knowing exactly what footage they would need, Universal had asked Ron as often as possible to film sharks swimming past without bars in the picture. I was frantic that he would take such a chance. By now there were three sharks around our baits, and Ron couldn't look everywhere at once. He was gambling on the other sharks remaining cautious while he concentrated on filming the more aggressive newcomer. Several times, watching from the deck, we saw Ron punch the shark in the mouth with his camera. Later Ron explained that his tank had become hooked over a metal bar on the hatch, stopping him from moving inside the cage as the shark approached. Not used to aggression, particularly in the form of a cold, hard camera housing, the white simply pushed Ron and the cage aside. The fish must have been surprised, but it did not appear at all intimidated.

Eventually, Carl was ready, and set out with Rodney in the nineteen-foot runabout *Skippy*. Rodney was adjusting Carl's mouthpiece when our new shark swam around *Skippy's* stern. The beast cut close to the hull, bumping the steel bridle attaching Carl's cage to the winch. Feeling the unfamiliar metal cable against his nose, the shark lunged blindly forward, pushing his great pointed snout further between the cables. Water flew. The *Skippy* rolled onto her side, dragged down by a ton of fighting fish. A huge head rose above the spray twisting and turning, black maw gaping in a frenzy of rage and frustration. Triangular teeth splintered as they tore at the restricting metal. The brute dove, his cycle tail whipping the air six feet above the surface.

Carl stood frozen with shock. As Rodney pulled him back, the shark's tail brushed Carl's face. Had Rodney been two seconds slower, the little stunt man could have been killed, his head crushed into pulp. As it was, the shark's tail had broken the hydraulic cables attached to the engine, and red hydraulic fluid was running across the deck. Carl looked down. "Is that my blood?" he asked. "No, it's oil from the broken cables," said Rodney. I had already grabbed Ron's movie camera and started shooting. Jim, who was holding an inch-and-three-quarter sisal rope attached to *Skippy*, had the rope snap in his hand, throwing him off balance and back into the drum of tuna mince. How Jim held against a pull hard enough to break a new 1,000-pound breaking strain rope I don't know, and neither does he, but many unusual things happened in that short space of time. Under the strain, the winch holding the cage on the surface began to bend. The shark's body crashed into the *Skippy's* hull, bouncing her across the water.

Again and again the fish tried to dive, mindless of the havoc above, striving only for freedom in the cold, dark depths below. Water was slopping over *Skippy*'s deck. One last time the shark rose above the surface, wearing Carl's cage like a monstrous necklace. The winch bent further. There was a loud cracking, and suddenly the *Skippy* sprang upright, minus her winch and part of the decking. A last mighty splash, then shark, cage, and winch vanished in a boiling, foaming swirl. Had Carl been in the cage, he, too, would have vanished with no possible chance of survival.

The *Skippy* sat quietly like a wounded bird. We were also silent, for there seemed little to say. Underwater, from his cage, Ron had filmed the whole thing, starting when the shark swam around the motors. Ron said that at first, because foam limited his vision, he had thought Carl must be in the cage. It wasn't until the shark, still entangled with the cage and winch, spun, twisting violently, towards the ocean floor, that Ron realized Carl must be safe.

It is a failing, this unshakable belief we have in the dangerous nature of sharks. How can they be a true threat, these creatures of the deep? They don't cast themselves upon the land to attack and devour, but remain living shadows in a world apart. We, in our arrogance, choose to enter their world, and with our uninvited presence, we cause some sharks to become a potential danger. Although the media would have us believe otherwise, very few sharks pose a threat to humans. Surprisingly, the largest of all sharks are plankton eaters, which is fortunate for us. Imagine a great white sixty feet long, swallowing everything in its path. Just the thought of such a fish makes me nervous, but the gentle whale shark swallows only plankton and small bait fish. Its trusting acceptance of humans is touching, though not well founded. The Asian lust for shark fin soup has become a serious threat to sharks worldwide, and the whale shark has the biggest fins of all. It seems a terrible thing to kill an elephant for its tusks, but no more terrible than killing these largest of all fish for their fins, dumping the unwanted body back into the ocean. When the last whale shark lies rotting finless in the depths, pictures like these will be all that remain, a tragic reminder of what we once had, and through our own greed and apathy, in one person's lifetime, lost.

The writhing mess was headed straight for Ron, who had a few moments of real fear before the whole lot plowed into the bottom, only a few feet away, stirring the sediment into a billowing mushroom of obliterating sand. Ron continued to film, and captured the shark suddenly darting away from the turbulence. By a miracle it had struggled free of the cage.

Once things quieted down, Carl returned to the *Trade Wind*. He seemed somewhat shocked. I saw him drag himself into the deck toilet, and push among the buckets and brooms which were stored there. The door was sliding open and closed as the vessel rolled over the swells, and thinking Carl deserved a little more privacy, I rammed a screwdriver behind the door, jamming it shut. During the following excitement, Ron had to rescue the cage, and we had to rescue Ron, not a fast process. Rodney was busy with his damaged boat, I was filming, and that I had Carl locked in the toilet went out of my mind.

Ron managed to retrieve the cage and winch by tying both onto his own cage so that all could be dragged back to the *Trade Wind*. He actually moved his cage along by putting his feet through the bars lifting up the cage (in much the same way as a woman picks up her petticoats) and walking it across the ocean floor, a safe but slow process. Two more sharks hovered like vultures, following Ron's every move. Whether just curious or awaiting a chance to attack, Ron couldn't say, but they stayed close. Ron had hoped to make a quick dash to the small cage and attach it so it could be pulled in separately, but with two sharks still around, it was too risky. It wasn't until sometime later, when the whole lot was physically dragged aboard by the men, that Ron told Jim he had shot the entire drama from start to finish. Jim was delighted with this news, and could hardly stop smiling. Dick asked where Carl had vanished to, and I suddenly remembered jamming the toilet door.

A feeding whale shark is an awesome sight. My nephew Jonathon Heighes is dwarfed by the open mouth. Although it looks dangerous, should Jonathon accidentally get in front of the shark, it will immediately close its mouth, for they eat plankton and small fish, not anything so large as a human.

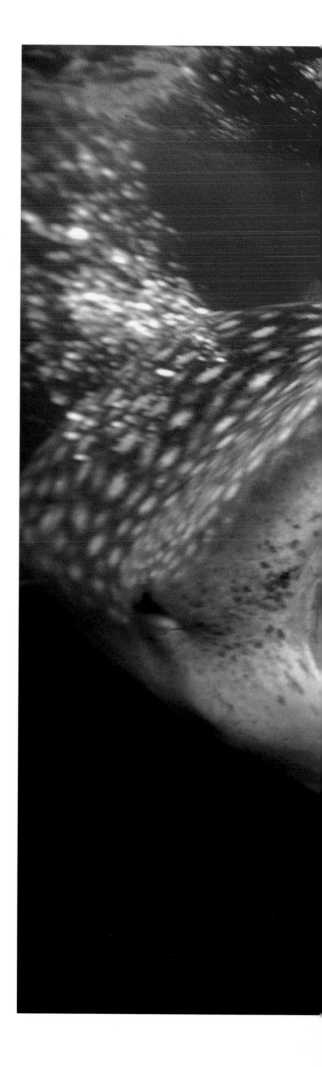

Poor Carl. He could just reach the very high window (too high to see in) with his hand. I could see it sort of clawing at the glass. I pulled out the screwdriver, and the door slid open. The small, stuffy, enclosed space had made him terribly seasick. He had broken out in a rash, and his voice had been reduced to a husky whisper. He went into the cabin and sat, a sad, gray shape, holding his head in his hands. I gave him a cup of coffee and a seasick tablet, but he never touched them. He just wanted to go home.

After dinner we headed back to port. The following day Jim left to have the film processed, then sent to Universal in Los Angeles so director Steve Spielberg could see what had been shot up to date. On the afternoon of March 5, we received word that they loved Ron's footage; the cage breakup was fantastic, but they would like more passing shots left to right and right to left if possible. More shooting lay in front of us, but we had proved that we could turn great white sharks in the wild into actors on the Hollywood screen.

The amazing success of *Jaws* and the realistic way it was presented left sections of the general public a bit hysterical. Popular beaches were almost deserted. Gung-ho macho men went around killing every shark they could find. The veritable shark mania following the release of *Jaws* pushed Ron and me and everyone else connected with the film into the international public eye.

When *Jaws II* was later completed, Universal had Ron and me tour the US, doing publicity television appearances. It was quite an experience for us and quite an eye-opener regarding the public's insatiable desire to know more about sharks—a desire that we found odd regarding the very remote danger that sharks present to most people. Strangers would stop me in places like Washington, DC, or in the local supermarket to ask me about the danger of sharks. The favorite question seemed to be, "What should we do if we are attacked by a shark?" Usually we would advise people to keep calm and if possible leave the water, advice that would have little use in a real attack. First, a shark attack is such a rare occurrence it's not worth worrying about, and second, no matter what I say, if someone is attacked by a shark, it would be all over before they could even realize what was happening to them, let alone remember what I had said. Having been bitten on three occasions, I know how fast it happens. Also, as someone with an unusual amount of experience in dealing with sharks, how I handle a shark attack can hardly be used as a blueprint for how a member of the public should handle it.

Jaws, as we all know, was a tremendous box office success. The giant shark is depicted at his ferocious best, eating his way with unflagging gusto through everything that crosses his path. At no time did we ever think that this film would have so huge an impact on the general public. It was a fictitious story about a fictitious shark, and there was never any reason to feel it would ever be considered as anything different. We are proud to have been part of the team that produced this film and remain forever amazed at the worldwide reaction it caused.

We come from the sea; salt water flows in our veins. It is our beginning, our birthplace, the mysterious soul of our planet. Unaided, our visits are brief but beautiful. Beneath its surface the clumsy are graceful, the cripple moves unaided, the old become young. We have, for a moment, returned to the womb; we are alone with the beating of our hearts.

The coastal people of Papua New Guinea rely heavily on the sea as a source of much needed protein. This young Trobriand Island boy from the village of Kiriwina is adding to the family food supply by spearing small fishes. It will take several small fish to make a meal, and this hunter will probably spend many hours in the water. The introduction of modern fishing techniques has decimated many of the once rich fishing reefs. It is difficult to explain to a young boy like this that overfishing could eventually mean no fishing.

For years I thought nothing could be more fun than coaxing a fish or shark to pose for my camera. However it usually took a great deal of patience and skill before they would start working with me, and there was always the possibility of their suddenly swimming away, leaving me feeling very cross at all my wasted effort. Then I discovered girls. They are easier to work with than fish and much more obliging, and I don't have to keep feeding them either, at least not while we are underwater!

Saving The Potato Cod

I shall never forget my first encounter with a Cormorant Pass potato cod. The creature appeared immediately after I descended, and as is their custom, rushed over for a closer look. It hung motionless, right eye six inches from my mask. Not happy with what he saw, the animal swung around and tried his other eye.

That didn't solve his problem either. Fat lips plucked at my mask, my hair, my arm, my leg. The fish was feeling me in the only way a creature without hands can. Several other rotund shapes hung weightless in the water, watching. I scratched the protruding bottom lip. The big eye swung down to inspect this unusual event. I patted his head. A big mouth swung up and sucked the offending member. I froze. The fish chewed it a little, then spat it out unhurt. I loved that fish; in fact, I loved his entire family.

It was July 1973 when Ron and I found the cod (actually a grouper). We were accompanied by several other divers. Although it was obvious that the fish were very friendly, one of the divers, wanting to impress his companions, speared a cod down the throat. The fish was not killed, but it was seriously hurt.

Ron was horrified. "We should try to remove the spear," he said. "The fish might survive without it, but has no chance the way it is now." It was a terrible business removing the spear. The flanges had opened deep inside the body and, understandably, the fish would not hold still. Finally, the weapon sort of twisted free, but the cod was weak, and blood constantly oozed from its gills.

We stayed with the fish for about five hours, taking turns holding him upright and gently walking him around, but he had been mortally wounded. Watched by us and members of his family, the cod eventually died. We left him there, eighty kilos of lifeless flesh, lying on the coral surrounded by his comrades. It was not a happy sight.

In 1973 no one lived on Lizard Island, and we were the only people who knew about what we chose to call our Cod Hole. Back at our camp on the beach at Lizard, Ron noticed with satisfaction that our spearfishing companions had marked the cod hole on their charts about thirty kilometers north of Cormorant Pass, its true location. "That's good," said Ron, "they won't be able to find it again." Ron was right; after three attempts, always looking in the wrong area, our companions became convinced that the fish had moved away and stopped searching.

Because fishermen love killing big fish, we decided not to visit the Cod Hole again.

In 1969, during the filming of *Blue Water White Death*, we had told some spearfishermen about our discovery of a similar group of potato cod off the island of Europa in the Indian Ocean. The spearfishermen chartered a fishing boat, and in six days they had slaughtered almost every cod in the area. With this thought in mind, we avoided going anywhere near Cormorant Pass and the potato cod for six years.

In June 1979, we desperately needed some dramatic footage for an hour-long television special we were shooting for Time Life. Strong winds had whipped the ocean into huge swells,

On June 29, 1986, Valerie Taylor was knighted by Prince Bernhard of the Netherlands at a reception in the Paleis Soestdijn, in Holland. This great honor was in recognition of her work for the protection of coral reefs and their inhabitants. In English, her title reads: Valerie Taylor, Knight of the Order of the Golden Ark.

and working on the outside reefs, where most of the large fish dwell, was impossible. We were running out of time, so with four days left of our charter, we returned to Cormorant Pass.

We were greeted like old friends, the fish swimming up to meet us as we entered the water. The resulting movie footage became the highlight of our television special. Unfortunately, the location of the Cod Hole, thanks to the charter boat skipper, also became public property. Cruise boats started taking tourists to swim with and dive around the fish. The cods' pictures appeared in overseas magazines, eating from a diver's hand. They also appeared dead, hanging from a fisherman's line.

In August 1981 we were in Cairns, Queensland, loading our boat the *Reef Explorer* for a filming trip to the Cod Hole. As we were preparing to leave, Peter Bristow, a local big game fisherman visited us. Peter was extremely angry. "You know those cod of yours?" he said. "Well, you won't find so many now. Some boat skippers have been taking clients to the Cod Hole for the fun of hooking or spearing those big fish." Peter said a lot more about fishermen catching, killing, and then dumping fish back into the water. It seemed that for a few moments of pleasure, several unscrupulous charter boat owners were taking their fishing parties to the Cod Hole, promising them the biggest catch of their lives.

During the October 1981 game fishing season, Peter Bristow feared the surviving cod would be destroyed. We left at once. After sixteen hours sailing, we dropped anchor off the northern end of Number 8 Ribbon Reef. As usual, the cod met us in midwater. Several wore hooks in their mouths; others had torn jaws where the fight against fisherman had been successful; others were no longer there. Marine animals, when unmolested by humans, are far more trusting than their above water counterparts, but these cod are trusting to the point of stupidity. They followed us like puppies, poking their fat lips into everything, eyes rolling in amazement. Ron's camera lens received much attention, for they could see their own reflections and seemed fascinated by the strange eye, so similar to their own, peering back from his lens.

We loved diving with our fishy friends, and did not want to leave so soon after arriving, but I was desperate to return to Sydney. Their number had been reduced by half; only twelve adults remained. I had to induce the National Parks officials or the local government to protect not only them but also their habitat, or they would disappear forever. I decided to ask for a pi (a circular kilometer) to be totally protected, which, in 2,000 kilometers of reef, seemed a very modest request.

However, the Queensland Government and the big game fishermen fought against me with surprising ferocity. They were not very honest about it either, but the conflict promoted more media attention, which I used to the best advantage. It was frustrating work. People in positions to help me proved reluctant to do so. It is easy to have a sweet-faced wallaby or a cute little bear protected, but a big, fat-lipped, slimy fish somehow is not considered quite as important. Eventually, after spending many fruitless hours begging government ministers concerned with environment and conservation for help, I turned in desperation to the media.

Television, probably more for the newsworthy controversy than the desire to do a good deed, became my greatest ally. Ron's footage showing me surrounded by the potato cod was a smash hit. Letters poured in to the Great Barrier Reef Marine Park Authority, all of them demanding action be taken to save the remaining fish before it was too late.

Events began to move swiftly. On August 18, I approached the editor of *The Bulletin* (a magazine similar to *Newsweek*), who suggested I tell Queensland and federal authorities that *The Bulletin* intended to publish an article about the government's lack of interest in protecting a species so rare it was not mentioned in a single Australian fish book. Much to the anger of the game fishermen, my request could no longer be ignored. On September 18, Graeme Kelleher, chairman of the Great Barrier Reef Marine Park Authority, phoned *The Bulletin* to say that the Potato Cod matter would be raised at the Great Barrier Reef ministerial council's next meeting. So *The Bulletin* delayed publishing its article. Senator Flo Bjelke Petersen, wife of Queensland's premier Jo, rang to assure *The Bulletin* she would urge her husband to protect the cod. On September 28, the ministerial council sent Ian Wilson, the minister for Home Affairs and the Environment, the recommendation that the cod's habitat should become a marine park. On October 30, the federal executive council, headed by the Governor General, gave me my pi. I was elated.

The cod got their one kilometer circle of total protection, and the government officials concerned looked like nice guys. Peter, Ron, and I were happy. It is a pity about the sports fishermen, but they still had hundreds of kilometers of unprotected reef to plunder of fish life, so they eventually stopped complaining. The victory is a high point in my life. It proves what an incredible country Australia is. Where else could someone, in ten weeks, cause the government of a great nation to pass a law to protect a small group of fat-lipped fish?

Ron and I are constantly working for conservation of the marine world's inhabitants, not only in Australia, but in all the oceans. It is a never-ending process, and often a disheartening battle, particularly where greed is concerned. The ocean's riches are free for the taking. No one has to farm the fishes and crustaceans; nature does that for us. I believe that our right to visit and enjoy a rich, life-filled reef environment is equally, if not more, deserving than the right of fishermen to destroy the same environment for their own personal pleasure or gain.

Alive, the potato cod can give hours of delight to thousands of people for decades. Dead, they give a few moments' fun, and only to the perpetrator of their demise. The fish I fought so hard to save have become a major tourist attraction on the Barrier Reef, and one of the best known. They bring millions of tourist dollars into Cairns and untold joy to anyone fortunate enough to visit them in their natural habitat. I find it very interesting that the organizations who originally refused to help Ron and me in our fight for the Cod Hole now proudly proclaim it as their own. Yet they still refuse to support our fight to protect other equally amazing and important marine wilderness areas that are under serious threat from over-exploitation. It seems that with the bureaucrats, experience is not the best teacher.

Sea turtles, unlike fish, close their eyes when they sleep. Loggerheads in particular like comfortable sleeping quarters and often rest their heads on soft coral, using it in much the same way that we would use a pillow. It is very pleasing seeing big turtles any time, but there is something heartwarming in the way certain individuals rest their funny old heads on the softest coral they can find. This "sleeping beauty" has chosen a semisoft, black coral tree as his pillow. Both the coral and the turtle lived on a wreck where we were filming an hour-long television documentary. Every time we worked at night, we would find several male loggerheads sleeping this way. They would become quite cross if we woke them up, banging into us or tangling themselves in the light cables. Fortunately, these antics would only last as long as it took to find a new bed and another pillow; then they would settle down as though nothing out of the ordinary had happened and go to sleep immediately.

A hatchling's first swim. She made it from her nest under the sand, down to the water without mishap. Now she has to survive, a tiny speck of life adrift in a hostile ocean. In fifty years' time, provided she is lucky, this baby turtle will return to Heron Island, and like her mother did nine weeks ago, drag her heavy aquatic body out into an alien environment, where she will dig a nest and lay her eggs. No one knows exactly where baby turtles go after birth. It's incredible, really, that with all our scientific knowledge, we still have to discover where little turtles spend the first years of their lives. Ron and I think the Great Barrier Reef hatchlings swim south, with the current, turning out into the Coral Sea somewhere off the coast of New South Wales. We have often gathered up hatchlings who have wandered inland and released them at sea. Always they swim south. I have spun them around, pushed them in other directions, but they turn south again. Even juvenile turtles, six months old when released from captivity, do the same thing. Every instinct in their little bodies says "south." There has to be a reason for it, doesn't there?

We found this turtle drifting out to sea. She had died from exhaustion after laying her eggs just at the waterline on Raine Island. The rising tide picked up her body and floated it into deep water, I slit her belly with my knife, then Ron and I followed, hoping the blood would attract a tiger shark. We were disappointed; the carcass attracted a shark all right, but not the hoped-for tiger. This shark is trying, without success, to bite into the turtle. Not quite the type of action we hoped for, but better than nothing at all.

This photograph has puzzled many people. The bottom turtle is a female and the two top ones are males. The middle turtle is having a good deal of luck. The top turtle is having no luck at all, but he's trying. It's just that he hasn't got the whole procedure clear in his mind. Perhaps it's his first affair. What he lacks in experience he certainly makes up for in endeavor. He thinks he's doing the right thing. The poor female! She has to carry those two great lumps around on her back. They don't swim: they just hang on and have a good time. This went on for about half an hour, and they did not split up. She had to breathe air, which meant surfacing; and when she surfaced, she had to push those two lazy males out of the water in order to get a breath of air. You can see the male's long tail, which contains his sexual organ.

Unlike green turtles, who feed mainly on weeds, loggerhead turtles are carnivores. I think the name suits them well, for their heads really are quite enormous. If annoyed, they are capable of biting their aggressors with their powerful, sharp-edged mouths—a defensive characteristic I have not noticed in other species of sea turtle. Perhaps because they have less to fear, loggerheads are more easily approached in the wild.

This big beauty had taken up residence under the Heron Island bommie where she slept the days away, waiting for nightfall to swim ashore and lay her eggs. We were shooting a segment for an English feature film starring Glenda Jackson and Ben Kingsley. It was called The Turtle Diary, and the script required several beautiful shots of a turtle in midwater. It was important that the amphibian give the on-screen impression it was swimming hundreds of miles through the open ocean.

As it was early summer, finding turtles was no problem, but to get them swimming at a steady pace in midwater was almost impossible. Then we discovered our loggerhead. She must have been the world's most contented turtle, for she swam slowly and steadily in midwater every time I woke her up. After swimming for ten minutes or so, she would return to her cave under the bommie, and very definitely not repeat the performance until she had slept for about forty minutes. However, forty minutes later, after a gentle shake of her flipper, I could ease her out and she would repeat the performance. It was really amazing. We worked with her off and on for five days, repeating the action at least twelve times. I offered her food, but she wasn't interested. She allowed me to remove several barnacles from under her left front flipper, which I could see were chafing, but no amount of persuasion would let me chip away at the one on her nose. (Interesting note—those particular barnacles are only found growing on sea turtles.) Because she was so obliging, we also did some still photography with her. In this picture, Ron is using his big 35mm Camaflex camera to shoot one of the scenes for The Turtle Diary. If the scientists are correct, in three years time, this old female loggerhead will be back here to lay her eggs again, and as I plan to be back as well, it could be an interesting meeting.

The Great Shark Suit

A n oceanic blue shark's mouth represents one of nature's marvels. Its rows of triangular, serrated teeth grip and tear flesh with amazing efficiency. This formidable sawtooth design has been tested over hundreds of millions of years of evolution and lies at the root of man's fear of this marvelous predator. The jaw in which these teeth sit also has evolved so that it can open nearly 180 degrees, allowing a shark a better chance of getting an effective grip on its prey. From a human point of view, a shark's mouth is perhaps the very last place you would ever wish yourself to be, but then at the moment, that's where I happened to be, with my arm in a blue shark's mouth.

It was June 26, 1980, twenty-five miles off San Diego on a clear day. Jeremiah Sullivan had joined Ron and me to test a protective suit of lightweight steel mesh. In 1967 Ron had observed a diving companion wearing a steel mesh boning glove sometimes used by butchers to protect themselves. He said at the time, "Valerie, if we could use this material to make something like a wet suit, I don't think a shark could bite through it." A dozen years later Ron had designed such a suit, and after initial trials in the Coral Sea, we had come to San Diego, hoping to test our suit against oceanic blue sharks (*Prionace glauca*).

The firm that manufactured the mesh boning gloves, Whiting and Davis in Plainville, Massachusetts, had constructed the suit from a material known commercially as mailite, a modern version of the medieval chain mail armor that became useless with the advent of the crossbow. This novel garment was still in the experimental stages, but with the addition of mesh gloves, I felt quite happy with my new armor. On this day, the pants of the mesh suit wouldn't fit over my quarter-inch wet suit, so I decided to wear only the top half of the mesh. I felt I could control the situation well enough, but I had forgotten the cardinal rule of shark bites: you never see the one that gets you.

In the open ocean, the oceanic blue is a known attacker of humans, and, unlike so many other members of its family, quite fearless around divers. We had been chumming with minced mackerel for two hours. The *Sea World*, owned by our friend Milt Shedd, drifted lazily on the Pacific swell. Sharks came and went, blue against blue, circling, their black eyes expressionless as a dead man's. We had been waiting, Jeremiah in Ron's mesh suit, me in my jacket, and Ron unprotected, camera ready. Although our initial tests had indicated that shark's teeth would not penetrate the mesh, learning to present myself for a shark to bite left me nervous. Some deep instinct for self-preservation had me pushing the sharks away, defending myself even when I wanted the attack to take place.

I was floating on the surface when a big blue caught me unawares and latched onto my arm with a sudden thump. I was startled, a natural reaction to seeing a neat set of razor teeth grinding into one's body with mindless fury. The nictitating membranes flicked back for a second as the shark looked at me; an eye black as ebony, gazed into my two blue ones. As the shock wore off, I realized that there was no blood, and that it wasn't really hurting. After the shark let go, my courage flowed back. The suit worked!

Now I allowed the arriving sharks to bite at will, which they did with only the provocation of the fish in my hand. I felt powerful, indestructible. My meshless legs received a certain amount of unwanted attention, so I kept them moving to discourage any attempts at biting, but in all I was feeling quite confident when a hard whack to the behind had me leaping from the water at full speed. A blue had nipped my unprotected rear, and only my fast movement forward had saved me from a more serious and rather undignified injury. As it was, three teeth had penetrated the neoprene of my wet suit, though the scratches on my skin were insignificant. The greatest damage was to my confidence, which was perhaps a good thing, for I was becoming careless and had not seen the shark.

The next day Ron, Jeremiah, and I entered the water together. The sharks were now larger and more numerous, and I was quite conscious of the risk I was taking by wearing only the top half of the suit.

The first shark came quite casually, eyeing the mackerel I was offering. As the nictitating membrane rose to cover its eyes, I withdrew the fish and offered my arm. The shark tore at my elbow, chewed down to my wrist, and munched on my hand. I thought, "My hand is unprotected except for the mesh." I waited for the blood, I waited for the pain. There was none. Just wrenching and pressure. I beat the shark away, and it was as if it had never happened.

Ron filmed on, the sharks circled, and history was being made. Another took a fish from my hand, and another grabbed my left arm. She began vibrating in the manner of most triangular sawtooth sharks. There was pressure but no pain, though I must admit to a prick or two where her very fine lower teeth penetrated the mesh. Being pulled about was unpleasant, as I lacked the strength to hold my own. Time and again I allowed the sharks to maul my arms. Several, unnoticed, initially chewed elsewhere on my suit. One even nuzzled up under my arm in a fruitless attempt at reaching a vulnerable part.

Ron was out of film quickly, but I stayed in the water so Jeremiah could take still pictures. Within a minute, one of the larger sharks approached unnoticed from above, grabbed me by the head, and shook me back and forth briskly. It was an absolutely horrible moment. Water leaked into my mask, as I struggled to repel my attacker.

Jeremiah stopped taking pictures and began beating the shark's head with his camera, which fortunately had the desired effect. The unexpected shake-up left me dazed for a few seconds, and just as I began to recover again, I found a shark suddenly chewing on my arm, which set me moving once more. My arms had never fully recovered from beating away the sharks in *Blue Water White Death*, and were becoming painful in the joints from so much pulling around. I knew my neck was going to have a problem, but I did not feel bad enough to leave the water. Although my legs received the occasional bump, the sharks definitely concentrated on my torso, probably because I was holding a whole fish in my hand.

Ten minutes later Ron was back with a freshly loaded camera. Several good blues came in, sunlight rippling over their bodies. I tried to let only the largest sharks bite me as they would look better on camera.

Two or three nice specimens swam close, eyeing my fish longingly, but they refused to attack. I felt sure that they were our first sharks and had learned through experience that there was nothing to be gained by trying to eat this strange, hard-shelled creature. As I tried to force

my arm into their mouths, they clamped them and their gills tight. From what we have seen, sharks, like many wild animals, learn very quickly from experience. In fact, we believe that sharks can learn a simple lesson faster than most other marine animals, particularly if motivated by food. Fortunately, several newcomers came up from the depths and did all of the right things. One even chewed around my chest without causing any problems, but I had to kick several away from my legs. By now I was beginning to feel cold, and it was with relief that I saw Ron indicating that he was out of film. Cold tends to slow down my concentration, and my reflexes become sluggish. Instead of sharks, I start thinking of hot showers and coffee, which can prove very dangerous.

Back on board, everyone was very excited. Against small to medium-sized sharks, the suit definitely worked. We had discovered a method of protecting a person against not only possible shark attack, but also attack from other dangerous marine and land creatures.

Ron and I are not scientists, nor do we seek any acclaim for our experiment with the mesh suit. The idea is an old one we simply updated and put to a different use. We had proved that wearing a mesh suit gave protection against shark attack, which makes what happened next all the more astonishing.

Two days after our successful testing of the mesh suit, our friends Howard Hall, Marty

The human race owes its incredible advancement to its hands. It would be useless having an intelligent brain without the ideal physical adaptations to put intelligence into practice. While the link between our hands and brain is unique in the animal kingdom, other creatures also use the sense of touch to help them better understand a new experience. We have all seen a cat reach out with a paw to feel an alien object before giving it closer inspection.

The blue shark in this picture has been lured up from a great depth for the purpose of testing our mesh suits. It has never encountered anything like me before. Most sharks feel with the tip of their noses before biting (white sharks are one of the exceptions), but they are, as this amazing picture shows, also capable of feeling with other parts of their bodies. So gentle was this blue shark's approach, that I am completely unaware of it directly above me. The other diver can be seen trying to signal to me that the shark is on my head. The fish is feeling me, touching—as you or I would touch—using his sensitive pectoral fins to do it. In fact, this shark has seen me, become curious, decided to find out more, preferably without me knowing, and has deliberately moved in above the limit of my vision to give me a gentle feel. If he decided I was harmless, and possibly edible, the next step would be a bump or bite. We have often noticed sharks, particularly whitetips, feeling with their bodies, but never before have we managed to capture the act on film so well.

Snyderman, and Fred Fisher joined Ron and me on the San Diego dive boat *Sand Dollar.* We were to shoot a sequence on shark behavior for an Alan Landsberg television production called *Amazing Animals,* one in which I was to show how easily I could coax a shark to perform for Ron's camera. To add interest to the sequence, I was to insert research tags in the dorsal fins of as many sharks as possible. As the mesh suit was not part of the story, although I had it with me, I decided not to wear it. Also we did not want to give the idea to someone else until after our own television production, *Operation Sharkbite,* had been screened.

Howard and Ron were shooting underwater; Ralph White, who had worked with us earlier on a shark-tagging television special in the Caribbean, was the above water cameraman. Bill Johnson, owner-skipper of the *Sand Dollar,* moved us to a location southeast of San Clemente Island, where we were drifting in a thousand or more feet of water. A brisk breeze had turned the sea choppy. As I was suiting up, Bill came over and said, with a twinkle in his eye, "Valerie, now you be careful, you hear? I don't want anyone getting hurt, but I particularly don't want you getting hurt."

I answered, "I'll be all right, Bill. If anything happens, it's never to an old pro like me." Famous last words.

It was a sunny day, and underwater visibility was excellent. The number of blues attracted to our baits had been increasing all morning. Howard and Marty had been down checking the action, and on surfacing Howard addressed everyone, saying, "If you want my opinion, it's fairly dangerous down there. The sharks are much more aggressive than usual. Fred, will you suit up? Marty can't keep all of the sharks off me. They keep breaking through his guard." As Howard is an old hand at working blue sharks, I took this piece of information seriously.

The weather was worsening, and conditions could become difficult if we waited too long. Howard and the two safety divers were to dive first to film Ron and me as we entered the water. As usual, we divers were joking among ourselves. "Looks like I might film my first genuine shark attack today," said Howard, in his casual way.

"As long as it attacks you and not me, I don't mind," I answered.

Once Howard, Marty, and Fred had submerged, we threw a few nice mackerel chunks off the swim platform, drawing the sharks into the area where we would enter the water. I went first, followed by Ron.

The scene was stunningly beautiful. Down and out as far as we could see sleek shapes of blue cruised lazily about. There must have been in excess of forty sharks, ranging in size from four and a half to seven and a half feet. Howard, Marty, and Fred could be seen about thirty feet down, where Marty and Fred were busy with their short sticks beating away sharks.

The sharks seemed unusually persistent, but more curious than aggressive. As our exhaust bubbles shimmered in ever increasing spheres toward the surface, I watched a shark, attracted by their movement, snap uselessly at the silver shapes. Seconds later I was too occupied with my own snapping sharks to continue observing the bubble-biter.

Sharks constantly approached, but I hit them away with the fish I was carrying. I wasn't worried; in fact, I was pleased, for conditions were superb and the action fast. I thought, "Wow! Alan Landsberg is going to get a super piece of film."

As I neared Ron, two good sharks came toward me, and I decided to feed one. I was concentrating on getting the composition of the shot right, using the mackerel as a lure to lead the shark toward Ron's camera lens. At the last moment, the shark lost interest. I must have teased him too long without a reward, for he swam away with a bored sweep of his tail. I was offering my fish to a second shark when I felt a thump to my lower left leg. Looking down, I saw a shark had it in his mouth.

Everything seemed normal. Howard with his plume of bubbles, Ron with his camera, the sharks. Even the one on my leg didn't look at that moment to be particularly out of place.

Instantly I began to hit the shark. I grabbed his nose and tried to push him off my leg. There was no horror or fear, just annoyance that the shark was so persistent. On the fourth hit, I saw the gum followed by the white teeth retract from the thick orange neoprene. Green blood gushed out clouding the water. I knew the wound was deep. I grabbed my leg, holding it tightly to stop the blood. My middle finger sank from sight swallowed by the wound in my calf.

pull the torn neoprene over the bleeding gash but it would not stretch enough.

enly, Howard was there, and Ron. I surfaced and called to the above-water camera art filming. I've been bitten, and I think it's deep." I found myself being escorted back

nd Dollar 100 feet away. Someone was helping me, Ron or Howard, I think, but I

ember too well. There was some difficulty getting me from the water, as the boat was

nd my leg was not working properly. I can recall demanding to climb the ladder by

ealizing I couldn't, then calling for assistance. Everyone was trying to help. Never

en so many worried-looking males. Blood, invisible on my red suit, spread in a

ol on the deck.

They laid me down and Ron held my leg up. I lifted up the torn piece of wet suit and felt sick at what was there. "All of that steak-looking stuff couldn't be my leg," I thought. Ron tried to roll back the suit leg to see the extent of the bite and stopped, horrified. He tried to cut the suit away with my knife, but it refused to penetrate the nylon lining. Someone handed him a sharper knife, and my lovely new suit was cut, ruined after only ten minutes of wear. "You've done it now," said Ron. "It's a bloody mess."

My leg looked horrible, but there was no pain. Howard immediately offered to stitch it up, but I wanted a plastic surgeon, not a diver. Weeks later I asked Howard why he wanted to stitch the wound. "It looked so awful hanging open. I just thought it should be sewn together quickly." It was a typical Howard Hall thought. Let's get the thing fixed.

Fortunately, the coast guard helicopter was in the air. With amazing skill they plucked me from the deck and flew me to the University Hospital in La Jolla. It was Dr. Mertzson Suzsuki, a fine plastic surgeon, who eventually sewed the wound with three layers of stitches, and except for a numbish foot, my leg today is almost normal. In three weeks I was back in the water working with sharks while Ron filmed.

It seems ironic that after dozens of bites I had received safely while testing the mesh suit, my very next dive without it should end so badly. While I was lying on the deck in a pool of my own blood, I can remember Ralph White, the above-water cameraman, saying somewhere in the distance behind me, "Don't worry. She's an Australian, and they are damn tough."

I don't know whether I am tough or not, but what happened to me was an accident. The shark did not attack me in the true sense of the word *attack*. It bit me, and there is a world of difference between an attack and a bite. Sharks in general merely bite people. If they attacked, few humans would ever survive, for sharks are kings of their environment, and we out-of-place visitors are essentially defenseless against their agility, speed, and razor teeth. I was fortunate. My shark was only a little larger than I. Had it been a four-meter great white, this story would have had a different ending.

The type of shark that bit me is an inhabitant of the deep waters of the open ocean, and they are rarely found close to beaches or human habitation. In the initial stage I sought out the shark, not he me; I certainly bear the shark no malice. We kept publicity about the incident to a minimum because I wanted the story told as it really happened, not with exaggeration or dramatics.

Ron and I will continue working with marine animals as long as we are able to dive. It's our living, our pleasure, our special way of life.

All my dives are too short. You get out of the water so quickly; it's all finished, and you have only just started. It's a glimpse into the abyss of the undiscovered, the unimaginable. It is an ancient place of unknown wonder.

Octopuses are among the most wonderful marine animals of all. The one pictured is small and very unusual; little is known about this species, for they are rarely seen. A friend of mine told me this story about himself and an octopus on a reef off the coast of Australia, where he was doing some film work on marine creatures. He would go out to film on the reef flats at low tide. Octopuses were fairly common. The local fishermen prized these little creatures to be used as bait, so my friend would spear any octopus he saw and save them for the fishermen. One day he speared an octopus but didn't kill it; the spear cut into the webbing that holds the base of its arms together, tearing a piece almost out. My friend said he, who thought he was the kindest of men, watched in shame and horror as the little creature picked up that piece of torn flesh and tried without success to put it back in the hole. I've befriended octopuses and been lucky enough to know some of them pretty well. They're just great, and it's a terrible pity that most people regard the octopus as some sort of slimy, eight-legged monster that likes nothing better than to suck the flesh from human bones. First, they don't ever grow big enough to successfully attack a human that way, and second, even if they were big enough, they are so shy and timid that they wouldn't do it anyway.

Sea snakes have a scary reputation they don't really deserve. Their venom is drop-for-drop more potent than that of the king cobra, and most people just don't like them. But if they would only get to know them, they're really friendly, placid, gentle creatures. They don't go around biting people; they can change their skin like an ordinary land snake, have a forked tongue, and scales: In fact, the main difference in appearance is that the sea snake has a flat, paddle-like tail, which makes it easy for him to swim. Almost all sea snakes bear live young, though two or three species go on land just to lay eggs. There are about twenty-eight species of sea snakes in the Indo-Pacific area. They don't have them in the Caribbean, and apparently don't want them either. Generally they mind their own business, but if they do come over to you, it's just curiosity. They're just thinking, "Goodness me, what a strange creature I have found!" I must add that Ron and I are very fond of sea snakes and enjoy their company.

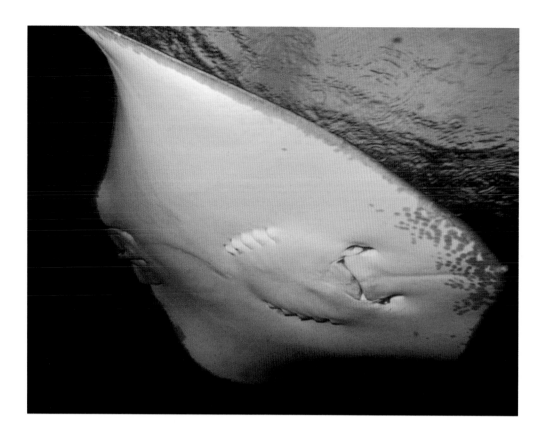

The waters surrounding Cocos Island, Costa Rica, offer innumerable opportunities for encounters with sharks and rays. This marbled ray swoops in close, giving us an unusually good look at its underside. In spite of its sinister appearance, the shark ray, below, is not dangerous to humans.

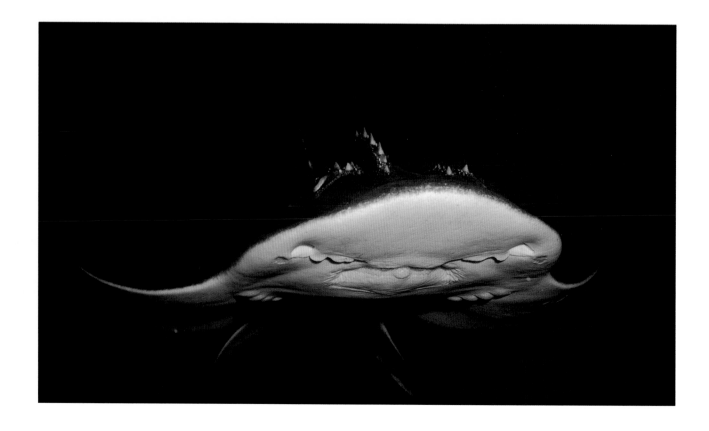

When darkness falls and fishes sleep, a new cast of characters emerges from hiding. They flit ghostlike across my beam of light, aliens from an unknown world, exotic inhabitants of a black sea.

Ron and I cannot decide what creature this is; we thought it could be a juvenile flying fish, but that is just a guess. I photographed it during a night snorkel. It was attracted to my light, and it stayed for about half an hour. I was swimming around the Reef Explorer, out of Low Island, Great Barrier Reef, at the time.

I also photographed the tiny fish below during a night dive at Luci Para, in the Banda Sea.

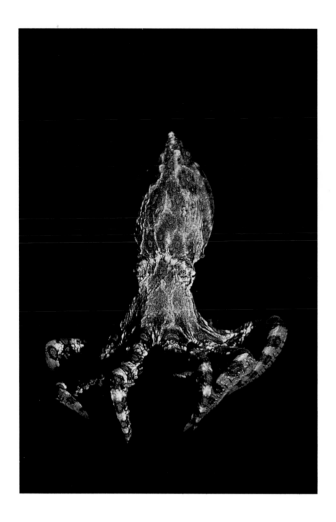

Found all around Australia, these shy but venomous little blue-ringed octopuses, while potentially very dangerous, have caused only a handful of human fatalities. They generally live under abandoned shells or rocks, well away from human contact. When disturbed, they glow with beautiful blue rings. This display of color is actually a warning, telling intruders to keep their distance. We found five of these lovely little creatures during one dive under the 110-year-old Tumby Bay jetty, Spencers Gulf, South Australia.

Observation Point, Milne Bay, is famous for weird marine creatures. This free-swimming nudibranch feeds by expanding its mantle (which contains its mouth) over the sand and scraping off food particles. Near dusk with barely enough light to focus, I found this wonderful little flamboyant cuttlefish, below, trotting across the sand in forty-five feet of water. I could not have been more excited if I had found a pot of gold. These magnificent cephalopods are rarely seen and even more rarely photographed. I spent a very happy hour following my new friend until lack of air forced me to the surface.

In between white shark trips, I photographed this gorgeous leafy sea dragon under the Tumby Bay jetty. Although difficult to find because of their superb camouflage and slow manner, they are easily photographed. Found only in South and Western Australia, leafy sea dragons generally inhabit shallow, calm water with an abundance of weed cover over a sandy bottom.

Perhaps this cuttlefish is telling me to keep my distance, but I feel that this display is a masquerade, to fool me into believing that it's not really there. Cuttlefish are among the most delightful of marine creatures. Their ability to change color, shape, pattern, and texture is equaled only by their close relative, the octopus.

I call this "The March of the Cleaner Shrimp," which is exactly what it is. These shrimp live in a small coral bommie which protrudes above a plain of sand in sixty feet of water. It is the richest and most diverse piece of coral I have ever seen. Along with two other species of shrimp and a family of labroides wrasse, they run the only cleaning station in the area. Fishes come by the hundred to be cleaned, making it a photographer's dream. The inhabitants are completely unafraid; if you put your hand onto the bommie, an army of shrimp will set to work on your skin, nipping and picking as though cleaning your hand is the most important thing in the world. Ron calls this bommie "a marine condominium."

Like a child licking its fingers free of crumbs after eating cake, this most beautiful of all the sea cucumbers uses its feathery arms to filter food from the water.

Ron, while using underwater lights to film marine life in the caves, found these beautiful little shells. We were surprised to discover it was new to science. Feeding primarilarly on corals polyps (pictured here), the wentletrap lives under shady overhangs throughout the Indo-Pacific, and grows to about one inch in length.

Seen during a night dive along a drop-off at Mai Island in the Luci Para group, Indonesia, this furry shrimp allowed me only one picture before darting back into the coral. I have only seen two of these shrimp in over thirty years of diving, both at night.

Night is the best time for seeing many species of bottom-dwelling creatures, particularly comical-looking hermit crabs. I did a series of photos showing anemone hermit crabs from every angle, because I needed them as reference for a children's book I was illustrating. The crab in the book is a vain villain called Warden, who not only collects anemones to put on his shell, but every other beautiful thing in the ocean as well. In reality though, hermit crabs usually settle for one particular species of anemone, as has this debonair fellow below.

We found this marvelous giant jellyfish about one mile from shore. Of course, we were in the water as soon as possible to take photographs. I likened it to a space ship. Traveling inside the bell were shrimps, crabs, small leatherjackets, and many other unidentifiable creatures. The hundreds of small fish following only went into the protection of the bell if they felt threatened, preferring to travel with, rather than in, this living transport vessel.

Only once have I seen this rare living nautilus. Its rough exterior covering is actually part of its shell.

The Shark Repeller

anuary 5, 1992, 5:15 A.M. phone call. Live shark in the nets. Mad rush out to sea. The mesh-
ers had a seven-foot zambezi (bull) shark tangled in the mesh nets off a popular surfing beach
just south of Durban.

Ron, film director Dick Dennison, topside cameraman Gordon Hiles, and I pounded
through the seven-foot swell in the Natal Sharks Board boat. The waves crashing on the
beach looked enormous, and I prepared for the possibility that we could broach and take
water, but the crew handled the surf superbly, and all I got was a little wet. The zambezi was
still very much alive when we reached the nets. Ron slipped in on snorkel and filmed underwater the tagging and release of the shark. Unlike their Australian counterparts, the South
Africans who run the meshing program are very conservation-minded. (In Australia the same
shark would have been killed and dumped). It was just the type of footage we wanted, and
we felt lucky to get it.

Then it was back to Sea World on the beach at Durban. I was to test a newly invented
device that, reportedly, created an electrical field that chased sharks away. Included in the
Sea World exhibit was a fine shark tank. We were to experiment on their captive zambezi
sharks. The Sharks Board had shown us a video of some tests they had conducted from above
water on a small shark in a small tank. Certainly the shark seemed upset by the field, but
because the pool was small, Ron and I felt that it only proved that the shark didn't like being
with electricity in an enclosed area. The shark tank at Sea World was very large and so
were the sharks who lived there, an ideal situation for testing the device.

The inventor, Graeme Charter, director of the Natal Sharks Board, and his technician,
Norman Starkey, were waiting when we arrived. They showed us a narrow plastic tube about
a meter in length. On closer inspection, we discovered it was full of batteries. There were two
strips of Velcro attached to the outside, one with a small magnetic switch attached to it.
Starkey said that by moving the magnet from one strip of velcro to the another, I could create
an electrical field that supposedly would cause a shark so much discomfort it would flee.
Ron muttered "Here we go again" and with good reason. Over the years we had tested dozens
of shark deterrent devices, all absolutely guaranteed to work. All had failed; experience suggested that this latest invention would be no different. And it really didn't look that impressive.

Ron and I entered the shark tank, and as these sharks are considered dangerous, I was
given a baseball bat to protect myself if the sharks reacted badly to our presence. It was, after
all, their territory. Ron and I acted respectfully. So did the sharks—fat, seven-to eight-foot
zambezis, four of them. There were also two saw sharks, one fifteen feet long, plus two beautiful big raggies or ragged tooth (gray nurse) sharks. We moved into position. The sharks
cruised past, not one foot away.

A female zambezi swam toward me; I activated the device. The shark flicked away immediately, as though stung by a bee. I zapped the next one and got the same reaction. I felt a sudden elation, for the stick actually worked exactly as Graeme had said it would. I discovered

I have met relatively few great hammerhead sharks in their natural environment, and only seriously worked with three. The fish pictured arrived under our charter boat in the Coral Sea, the Coralita while skipper Wally Muller was cleaning fish. Ron and I were on the top deck packing away our gear when Irvin Rockman, one of our diving friends, suddenly climbed onto the duckboard calling, "There's a big hammerhead around." Ron and I were in the water in minutes; at first we saw only a few little white-tips and thought Irvin was playing one of his silly jokes. Then suddenly a massive elongated head materialized.

What magnificence! Here was the king, and he knew it. We watched in delighted awe as the shark carefully circled our fish frames lying on the corals. Suddenly, with a fluid flick of his strange-looking head, he scooped them up, crunching through the bones as he swam away. I surfaced, yelling, "More bait, Wally, more bait," and was thrown a bucket of fish scraps. As the bloody muck sank down, I thought the shark might show some excitement, but he calmly swam around, observing us closely, before continuing to feed. I placed several fish carcasses directly in front of Ron, who filmed the most amazing sequences of the hammerhead eating. It showed no fear, but would shy away when touched, even very gently.

There has been much speculation as to why the head is so oddly shaped. Watching this shark, particularly around the bait, we saw him move his head from side to side, in what could well be described as a searching motion. Certainly the eyes, placed as they are on the ends of the hammer, would have a marvelous range, but he seemed to be smelling with his head, rather than using it visually. He swam very close to the coral. I had dragged several baits around, saving them for later filming. The shark picked up my trail, and although I was relatively close, followed my erratic course to and fro, before heading in my direction. If the hammerhead looks strange side-on, from the front he is almost scary.

Although blamed for attacks on humans in other parts of the world, there are no proven cases in Australia, and I personally don't consider the hammerhead to be a true attacker of people. Great hammerheads grow much larger than the records indicate (up to six meters), and are found throughout the tropical and subtropical regions; it certainly makes my day happy whenever I meet one.

Gray nurse sharks are also found along the South African coast, around Japan's southern islands, and in some areas off America, India, and China. I have seen four of these groups. Their differences are certainly not noticeable to my unscientific eye, yet each has its own scientific name. South Africans call their version of the gray nurse ragged tooth, and blame it for many attacks on humans. But in the USA the same shark is called a sandbar tiger and considered to be completely unaggressive if left undisturbed. In the state of New South Wales, these gentle sharks are protected, and I am proud to say that Ron and I played a large part in having this law passed.

that the device could cause the sharks to react in different ways. A big jolt would send them off in a spin, or I could give them a quick hit, which made them turn away in a more casual fashion. The extent of their responses could be controlled by the length of time that I kept the pulse activated.

While the device was in use, Ron and I felt nothing, nor did the other fish in the tank, which just kept swimming normally.

I never zapped the ragged tooth or saw sharks, only the potentially dangerous bulls or zambezis. After half an hour, I found that just the sight of me and the stick could make the sharks flinch. I didn't have to activate the power (which was twelve volts), for they had learned that my stick and I could cause them discomfort. After twenty minutes of not being hit, however, they started to believe that I was no longer a menace and swam closer. I waited until old wart nose (one of the zambezis carried a big wart on her nose) brushed my shins with her fins, then zapped her with amazing results. There was no doubt that the device worked. In fact, I began to feel a bit sorry for the sharks, who bore me no ill will yet suffered my harassment without retaliation.

January 6. Back at Sea World, Norman Starkey and Graeme Charter were once again waiting for us. By now, Ron and I were as keen to continue testing the invention as they were, for we realized that, provided the tests continued to go well, Graeme's shark repeller had an exciting future. This time we attracted sharks with live bait (mullet on a fine fishing line threaded through its dorsal fin). Just as the shark was about to take the mullet, Norman would zap it and cause it to flinch away. Ron and I watched from inside the tank as Norman activated the device from above water; it was most impressive. Norman tried all different powers, and only the weakest, at four volts, had no effect. Ron filmed the sharks as they were about to swallow the swimming mullet, and every time Norman zapped the shark, it flicked away, not a normal reaction for a shark about to take a fish. I began looking forward to trying it with great whites in the open ocean. If it could turn them, the Sharks Board had a real winner in its hands.

After the Sea World experiments, we again visited the shark protection nets that line the beaches off northeastern South Africa and found a spotted dolphin which had drowned before

My favorite tiger shark. We gave her a tuna which she swallowed whole. You can see the tail protruding from her mouth. Photographed at Coralita Pass, Marion Reef, Coral Sea.

the boat crew could set it free. It was exactly this type of bycatch that the Sharks Board people hoped to prevent with the device we were testing. In all, the people at the Sharks Board were very impressive. Many of them were Zulus, and I noticed that all of the whites spoke fluent Zulu. The majority of the boat crews were also Zulu, and better seamen would be hard to find.

Monday, January 14. Dyer Island, southeast of Cape Town. Ron, the film crew, and I were installed in an old, one-room stone house on the island. We had chartered an ancient fishing trawler for use as a work platform. The first day about nineteen white sharks came to our baits, of which three fed, but only on the dead seal we had been given by the museum. Water visibility was very poor. Ron spent over two hours in the cage and got one shot of a small (seven-foot) shark taking the bait and several passing shots of a twelve-to fourteen-foot male. These South African sharks came in all sizes. Their lack of interest in our baits was understandable, for they were feasting on pups from a huge sea lion colony on the southern half of the island.

One dear little fellow swam out to our boat. Goodness knows what he was trying to do—a little exploring, perhaps. Anyway, it was obvious to us that with so many sharks around, he was doomed. Sure enough a big fin broke the water behind the pup just as he was starting back to the island. He moved as fast as his little fins could take him. We all yelled; a great head broke the surface, and the little pup vanished in a swirl of water. The shark's tail thrashed, and then the pup reappeared, swimming hard. The white hit again with even greater speed, and once more little sealy vanished. All was still for nearly half a minute, then up popped the brave wee fellow swimming for his life. A third time the shark struck, and again the pup vanished. We all thought that was the end, but, to our amazement, the little pup reappeared. In apparent desperation the shark leapt from the water like a mako and hit the pup.

Water flew, blood flew, the big gulls swooped in for the scraps. The little seal was no more. The shark, some twelve feet long, thrashed around on the surface for a bit. Gordon filmed the whole thing; it was very dramatic but we felt sad for the pup.

Our tests at sea proved anything but easy. A storm with enormous seas tore loose our shark cage during the night, and it was swept away in the current, a major loss. After a day's delay, we had to make do with the heavier tiny cage from the Sharks Board. With a huge swell and a strong current running, Ron and I entered the cage. Immediately a shark started feeding on our baits. The surge kept bouncing the cage partly out of the water, forcing me into the crossbars. When other sharks appeared, watchers on the deck would yell to let me know. It was too rough to see anything from water level, and the visibility underwater, a hazy six feet, made it impossible for me to see the shark's reaction to Graeme's zapper, or for Ron to film it with his underwater camera. When I finally did see a white shark take the bait next to the cage, I zapped him. He seemed to go crazy, sort of standing on his head and lobbing his tail, with spray flying everywhere. The bait he swallowed reappeared, floating back into the cage. Although Theo Ferreira, our local shark expert on deck, strongly disagreed, I was sure that the shark had spat it out when he was zapped. Then a giant swell sent the cage reeling. My little finger became jammed between a join in the cage and was crushed. It wasn't painful at the time, but later I really suffered.

The barrier seemed to be working on the whites, but it was difficult to form a proper opinion. We knew the sharks were reacting but we couldn't see exactly what was happening, which was very frustrating. Also, I kept getting electric shocks. I was wearing the device on my back. One electrode was on my leg, the other on my arm. The mercury switch I held in my right hand. The bars of the cage seemed to be affecting the electrical field, and the surge continually forced me into them. During my long hours in the cage that day, I can honestly say that the zapper seemed to turn a great white on three separate occasions. The rest of the time I couldn't see enough to tell for sure. Once the zapped shark swam sideways, but not away, almost as though something were annoying its right side. When we were finished, the pounding in the cage had left me aching all over, almost as if I'd been beaten up.

Back on the boat, everything seemed chaotic. I was wet, cold, hungry, thirsty, sunburned, and hurting, but no one seemed to care. They were all running around in a mild panic. "What's happening," I kept asking. Dick Dennison finally told me "There's a big blow coming. We've got to get to shore." The sea was already so big that the thought of even bigger seas was genuinely alarming.

Dick, the film crew, and I took off in the small runabout, racing along like a bunch of mad lemmings, driven by huge waves and a screaming wind. I wanted a hot shower, my finger was hurting, and my shoulder was in pain as well. When we reached the jetty it seemed like heaven.

January 22. All of us were up early and pleased to see calmer weather. When we reached the boat, three sharks were feeding, but because of a mishap with his equipment, Norman had

Portrait of a captive gray nurse shark. It's one of many I took in Manly Oceanarium after I was asked for a picture of a shark with protruding teeth to use on the cover of a book. Gray nurses are easily found off the New South Wales coast, but to take a series of suitable portraits in the wild would have been impossible.

to use part of my device to get the above water repeller working again, leaving my zapper useless. Dr Leonard Compagno, the world's leading authority on sharks, had joined us for a few days and was waiting to observe the tests. Graeme Charters tied the electrode to a bait and floated it out. A shark came in slowly, its fin cutting the water. You could sense he was all excited and about to take the bait when Norman zapped him, a hit of about two seconds. Immediately the shark leapt from the water with a great splash, and shot off toward the horizon. Everyone cheered! Twenty-seven hits later, without a single miss, we all knew that the barrier worked well. Then came what seemed the ultimate test.

A little seal pup was swimming up to the boat. We all remembered the earlier death of the baby seal in the jaws of a great white, nature operating at her most distressing. When we started yelling, the pup—an innocent little thing—looked up in surprise, then turned and headed for shore. I was shouting, "Swim! Swim!" but pups learning to swim lack the speed and maneuverability to avoid a white shark. A huge fin broke the water about twenty feet behind the pup, and over the next few seconds, closed to within five feet. The great head started to break water, causing a bow wave that bore down at horrifying speed. The pup seemed doomed, then Norman zapped the shark. The pup and the shark were about thirty-six feet away from the boat, so we could see clearly what was happening. When the pulse hit, the huge fin veered away, sending a sheet of spray into the air. Our brave little seal swam safely onto the beach, and so impressed were we with the demonstration, we all cheered loudly.

Ron and I agreed that the behavior of these South African sharks differed from that of their Australian cousins. They never bit the cage or the boat, they were not as persistent around the baits, and they simply would not take the baits from the boat, preferring those floating some fifteen to twenty feet behind the stern. Moreover, they never once lifted their heads above water to look at us, which suggested that they had evolved with personalities dissimilar to those of Australian great whites. To my eye they also looked a little different, with bigger fins and a more pointed head.

Ron decided that to get useable underwater footage, we would have to try diving in the water with the sharks. Actually we didn't have much choice. With three days to finish filming and no cage, we had some hard decisions to make. George Askew, a South African cameraman and old-time spearfisherman, was to take down a second camera and film Ron and me together. P.J., another local, was to come in and protect George's back. I was to wear the personal protection device, but with its battery missing; I couldn't activate it (not that it mattered as we wanted to photograph sharks, not frighten them away). Above us Graeme would have a working barrier in place to zap any sharks around us if we ran into trouble.

When Ron and I jumped into the water, I discovered to my horror that the housing for the barrier attached to my back was too buoyant because the batteries had been removed. The current made it a hard swim back to the boat, and while I yelled for weights, it took those on deck about three minutes to get them for me. Meanwhile I was swimming around uneasily on

the surface, surrounded by floating baits and at least two sharks. Finally the weights arrived and I made it to the bottom.

George, Ron, P.J., and his menace of stick (about eight feet long) were all waiting for me. Although we knew sharks were around, the visibility of a hazy fifteen feet combined with the current and the surge made keeping together difficult. As if we didn't have enough problems, the stony bottom was covered with small, sharp-spined sea urchins. They were packed so tightly that I couldn't find any area to hang on to until I eventually discovered that I could hook my electrode onto a small rock.

The first shark appeared almost immediately, a little fellow about ten feet long. It was simply, suddenly there, only six feet away from me. No matter how big or how small great white sharks are, they are always impressive to behold. In murky water, on an uncomfortable bottom, they are more than impressive—awesome would be a better description. The shark, an immature male, passed without haste, a sedate and sinister torpedo of a beast, perfect beyond imagination. What he thought of us I will never know, but we all thought he was the most exciting animal we had ever seen. I guess it was the absence of a cage that made it so dramatic. P.J. kept pointing his stick at the shark. I felt we could have done without the stick; I had much more faith in the Shark Board's zapper.

The sharks came and went with easy assurance, mostly one at a time. With no way to see beyond fifteen feet and without a cage, we were all pretty high on adrenaline. Above on the boat, the crew could see much better than we, but they had no way to tell us what the sharks were doing. I identified three sharks, one the perfect male, another that had been tagged, and a female with a damaged pectoral fin. Ron had been hoping to shoot under a white shark taking a bait, but the current kept dragging us away, and the great whites showed no interest in the floating baits or in swimming on the surface as we expected them to do. Instead, they sank to the bottom where they could observe us better.

One of those rare occasions in the life of an underwater photographer when everything goes right. It was late afternoon; I was photographing a pair of sweetlip groupers when I looked up and saw this tawny shark swimming past. There was time to flash off only one shot before the shark disappeared. The shot is unusual because this species of shark generally swims along the bottom, not in midwater.

They appeared casually curious, but in no way threatening. Despite the urchins, I was enjoying myself. I could see Norman's barrier, a comforting but hazy silhouette, drifting overhead between the baits.

We had nineteen sightings or passes of great whites, the female with the damaged fin coming most often. P.J.'s stick was proving too long for him to handle easily and was causing problems for us as well. He would grip it halfway up, cutting a swath through the rest of us with the back of it as he swung it around at a shark. Sometimes a shark would be just a few feet away before we saw it, but mostly they came no closer than nine feet or so, turning aside the moment we made eye contact. At no time did I feel in danger or threatened, but even so, it was absolutely exciting, heady stuff. We were swimming with feeding great white sharks, without a cage, in the open ocean. We were doing the impossible.

When P.J. indicated that his air was running low, I surfaced and told Norman to activate the barrier, and we all scrambled out. On the platform it really hit home, and we all laughed and shook hands. Then I broke the news to my diving buddies: my zapper had not been working the entire time. They had gone in the water believing I could protect them if things got out of hand, but they took the news well, and we all laughed and shook hands some more. At that moment I loved everyone, and everything felt so wonderful.

Back on shore in our funny old hotel, we celebrated with a wonderful meal of fresh salmon and fine wine. Bad weather, a constant presence down on the cape, was rolling over the mountains. We packed up and left. Anything we now did would seem like an anticlimax after the Dyer Island dive. Dick was happy with his film. Graeme and Norman were happy because the device had worked successfully. Theo and Craig were happy because they had tagged over twenty sharks. It was a good ending.

Three days later we were on our way back to Australia; someone had at last invented a device that really did repel sharks, but it was a long way from being available to the general public. There was a lot more testing to be done.

In February 1992, Graeme Charter and Norman Starkey came to Australia with the latest prototype of the shark repeller.

Coral Sea, Australia, February 8. Marion Reef. Morning, sitting on the sand in twenty-five feet of water, clear and warm. Although we baited heavily, only seven whitetips approached. A few little gray reef sharks hung off in the distance. A big difference from the twenty to thirty sharks we had experienced before the sharkfinners had longlined the area. The whitetips certainly reacted to the barrier I was wearing, but only at close range. I would hold a piece of fish in the same hand as the electrode. The device was strapped to my chest, a far more convenient place than on my back. As soon as a shark started to chew on the fish I was holding, I would activate the barrier. The first pulse would cause the shark to roll his eye and flinch. The second would leave him noticeably uncomfortable, after which the shark would flick away, twisting and turning. I did this on six occasions. Eventually, none of the sharks

This small silvertip shark, with its following of jacks, has been attracted by fish carcasses tied to the reef. For most shark photographs, baits are essential, as without them the subject is there for only a fleeting instant, and getting a shot like this one becomes almost impossible.

would come to my bait. The zapped sharks had all shot away with great speed, one bumping his head on my elbow with such force that it hurt for days. But I was disappointed with the lack of range in the new prototype barrier. Only within a foot or so did the sharks react strongly. The pulse seemed to work much better from the front of the shark than the side. Ron patiently recorded the entire seventy-five-minute experiment on film.

2:00 P.M. Marion Reef, Coralita Pass. That afternoon we decided to test the big barrier, which Graeme and Alex Petersons, our assistant, strung along twenty-five feet from the coral wall to a coral table on the left side of the channel. We baited heavily, but left the barrier on, and as expected, nothing we could do would induce the sharks to feed. Eventually two of the sharks showed some interest, but another seven hung in deep water around the corner of the coral. They seemed unwilling to leave, acting as if they sensed danger but could not understand why.

After circling for three-quarters of an hour, two whitetips suddenly gained confidence, and while the barrier was still on, swam over and around it. Then I noticed that the electrodes were fizzing, not pulsing, indicating that somehow the long barrier had malfunctioned. Further testing would have to wait for repairs.

February 11, Action Point. We set out to test the large barrier again at Marion Reef's famous Action Point. Although the point was formerly home to over thirty gray reef sharks, that day, sadly, only two appeared, plus a lone whitetip. Once again the long barrier malfunctioned, but this time it was our fault for letting two electrodes touch. With the long barrier useless, I put on the middle-sized barrier and had the whitetip flicking and flinching from a distance of five to six feet. I also found out something about the sensitivity of sharks up close to the zapper. A whitetip swam directly over my head. I tried to zap it aiming at its stomach, but as far as I could see nothing happened. A minute later the shark was back, and this time I zapped it in the face from a closing distance of two feet. I was pleased to see him flick away instantly.

There was no doubt that the personal barrier worked well at close range. Also, after a few hits, the sharks became very respectful. But I was disappointed in our failure to test the bigger barrier. The fish and sea snakes who also came to feed at the baits were completely unaffected by the barrier, as were the divers. I was saddened, however, to see the decimation of the sharks and other marine life in this area. It seems a high price to pay for a bowl of shark fin soup.

November 23, 1992, North Reef, Capricorn Bunker Group. Ron Isbel, the skipper of the *Tropic Rover*, took us to North Reef, where we were diving in an area new to us. We had baited for three quarters of an hour, when a nervous shark appeared. I took three fish that my nephew, Mark Heighes, had speared and laid them on the sand in twenty-five feet of water. The shark made several passes, then dashed in, grabbed one, and started chewing it as she swam away. I swam after her, and when she slowed down to swallow the fish, I zapped her

for about half a second from around five feet. She twitched, covered her eye, and spat out the half-chewed fish. In thirty seconds she was back, suddenly very confident. She dashed in and grabbed the dropped fish. She started shaking her head. Bits of fish flew everywhere, so I zapped her again. She shot away once more, and this time didn't return for six minutes. Over the next forty-five minutes, I repeated this action seven times on two whaler sharks, both some seven feet long, driving them off each time.

The variety of circumstances in which we tested the barrier began to give us the data we needed and some clues about ranges and uses of the device. Along the way we witnessed some extraordinary results. Sharks seem to need a zap of at least one to three seconds before reacting strongly. Also, I found that I had to hold the zapper forward of the pectoral fins for best results. When the pulse of the barrier hits the shark, its whole body flinches, the gills snap shut on the side that the zapper hits, and the eye closes. The flinch always moves the shark away from the zapper. One shark I zapped as she swam directly toward me, and she did a most impressive back flip before speeding off into the distance. We were very pleased to see how easily the zapper instantly turned sharks, but they did not stay away, although had I left the zapper pulsing, they might have.

January 11, 1993. M.V. Telita, *Milne Bay, Papua New Guinea.* Today we tested the zapper on three occasions, each series of tests confirming what we had witnessed previously. The *Telita* was anchored on a submerged reef, the top of which finished forty-five feet below the surface. The deck crew had caught several tuna, which they filleted on the back deck. Blood dripping from the fillet table into a one-knot current quickly had three gray reef sharks at the swim platform.

Leopard sharks are bottom-dwellers. Generally shy around divers, they appear off the New South Wales northern coast during the summer months, migrating into warmer waters for the winter. The shark pictured lives near Lady Elliot Island on the southern Barrier Reef, and is frequently seen by divers. Leopard sharks lay raggedy-looking egg cases which they tangle into the bottom. Their young are beautifully marked and look more like a child's toy than a shark.

Ron decided it was a good time to try the zapper. Using a piece of tuna on a rope, we teased sharks in close. Each time a gray reef tried to take the bait (I would wait until it was in his mouth), I zapped him, a quick hit of up to five seconds. In every case the shark spat out the bait and dashed away, splashing on the surface as it went. Eventually no amount of baiting would lure them in close to the platform, though they continued to hover about fifteen feet out, swimming to and fro in the blood slick. Ron said, "I don't know what it does to them, but they sure hate it. Maybe it's like getting a nose full of ammonia."

Then we decided to take a string of baits down on a lead weight, with the baits suspended above the weight by a float. This allowed everyone to easily see and photograph the sharks. Eventually, after much chumming, two gray reef sharks began to feed. I let them go for about sixty seconds, then I swam in and zapped them. The reaction was immediate and dramatic. The sharks shot away, and no amount of baiting would bring them back.

After a break, we moved to another submerged reef where the *Telita*'s skipper, Bob

Halstead, often arranged a shark feed for his guests. We decided to see how the barrier would work in a feeding frenzy. Using tuna, the best bait of all, we had a full-blown frenzy underway in about twenty minutes, with nine gray reef sharks going at it full tilt.

I waited until the baits were two-thirds gone and the frenzy at its peak; then I swam in, turning on the zapper. The results were dramatic, and conclusive. The frenzy stopped abruptly, and the closest sharks fled. Unaware of any problem, other sharks dashed in from a distance only to jerk away, instantly, when they came within range of the zapper, which extended a good ten feet or more. In less than sixty seconds we had no sharks.

I switched off the barrier, and scraped tuna into the current. Once the slick was going well, I moved back, but the sharks kept their distance. They were still hungry, and they knew the food was there, but the unpleasant experience had left them unwilling to approach. I chummed for another three-quarters of an hour before leaving the water without a single shark even swimming close to the baits. In fact, Ron and I are a little embarrassed. Three years later Bob Halstead reported he still had not been able to coax these sharks back to feed again. The memory of the experience apparently has a powerful influence, for no matter how much Bob baits, they won't come closer than about sixty feet.

Ron and I feel no need to test the barrier further with gray reef sharks. Our latest test, an important one, took place in March 1995, when Ron zapped a feeding great white from the stern of the *Lonnie Clare* at North Neptune Island out from Point Lincoln, South Australia. The shark had been extremely active, but when hit, it thrashed on the surface in a crazy fashion, then did a vertical nose dive into the depths. We saw it again briefly, and that was all. It never returned, nor did any other sharks. In South Africa, the latest tests using the repeller against great whites repelled sharks continuously from a distance of eighteen to twenty-four feet. The device ran constantly and worked perfectly.

The shark barrier invented by Graeme Charter and developed by the Natal Sharks Board has been tested thousands of times with continued success. It is now emerging as a reality, signaling a turning point in mankind's enduring fear of sharks. The Sharks Board aims to eventually replace the mesh nets off the Natal coast with a barrier that will keep the beaches free of sharks yet allow other creatures access without harm. The present tragic loss of so many marine animals in the mesh nets will become a thing of the past, and armed with an effective personal protector, divers the world over will be able to enjoy the oceans without the fear of a shark attack. I can see where in the near future every life jacket, surf board, life boat, or seagoing craft will be fitted with a suitable version of this invention, and humans will no longer be able to offer the excuse that they are killing sharks to save lives as a justification for their desire to slaughter these magnificent fish.

From its purple depths to the glittering sun-spangled shallows, the sea sings its own song of life, love, and death. It seduces all who listen into a never-ending love affair. The great rewards do not come easily, but must be coaxed into your being like an elusive scent on a sea breeze.

You must learn to look beyond the veneer of color and movement, for beneath is a gift from the sea to be savored: two lionfish at sunset, orange tube worms feeding, or your beloved friend gliding toward a coral wall, elegant as any sea dweller. I have a storehouse of such treasures—some huge, some tiny—and all are precious, for combined, they have become the essence of my life.

There is a grandeur on this earth which is an inherent part of all nature's creations. It is in the song of the wind, the flight of a bird, the silent passing of a great predator. The shark in this mesh net did not need to die. It was destroyed, as so many of its kin have been, because we humans are afraid that at some remote time, in some faraway place, it could possibly be a danger. A day will come when the shark in the net will be the last of its kind. It's going to surely happen unless we stop our senseless destruction of the creatures with whom we share this planet. Greed is our master, apathy our crime. I have stood on the sand and seen perfection pass. I have felt a humble awe as the flat, black eye looked briefly into mine. I have climbed from the water, the adrenaline pumping, screaming with joy, and I ask myself if a child of tomorrow will ever experience the wonder I drank in that day.

Acknowledgements

Special thanks to my husband Ron, who built my camera housings, gave me support, wise advice, and most important of all, love.

To Michelle Warren, my wonderful secretary, who shouldered many burdens on my behalf, and kept on smiling.

I will be forever grateful to Charlene deJori and Cheryl Schorp. Without their faith in my talent as an underwater photographer, this book would never have been published.

To Bob and Dinah Halstead, who taught me to see the secret creatures of the sea.

And to Peter Gimble for *Blue Water White Death,* the greatest adventure.

IMAGE IDENTIFICATION:

Bob Halstead, who helped me identify many of my slides.

Dr. J. Paxton of the Australian Museum.

Dr. John Randall, Gerald R. Allen, and Roger Steene, *Fishes of the Great Barrier Reef and Coral Sea,* Crawford House Press, 1990.

Neville Coleman, *Encyclopedia of Marine Animals,* Angus & Robertson, 1991.

Bruce Halstead M.D., *Poisonous and Venomous Marine Animals of the World,* United States Printing Office, 1970.

Robert F. Myers, *Micronesian Reef Fishes,* Coral Graphics, 1989.

Robert H. Carcasson, *A Field Guide to the Reef Fishes of Tropical Australia and the Indo-Pacific Region,* William Collins Sons & Co., 1977.

Neville Coleman, *Australian Sea Fishes North of 30 Degrees South,* Doubleday Australia Pty. Ltd., 1981.

J.E.N. Veron, *Corals of Australia and the Indo-Pacific,* Angus & Robertson Publishers, 1986.

Isobel Bennett, *The Great Barrier Reef,* Lansdowne Press, 1971.

Frank Talbot, Roger Steene, Mead & Beckett, *Reader's Digest Book of the Great Barrier Reef,* Reader's Digest, Sydney, 1984.

Walter Deas, Steve Domm, *Corals of the Great Barrier Reef,* Ure Smith, Sydney, 1976.

Plate Notes

2/3   Blue shark, *Prionace glauca*, San Diego, California

4   Cousteau shark cage, Con Shelf at Shaab Rumi reef, Red Sea

7   Whitetip reef shark, *Triaenodon obesus*, Marion Reef, Coral Sea

9   Picinniney Ponds, Picinniney Chasm, South Australia

11   Valerie and purple anthias, *Pseudanthias tuka*, Northern Great Barrier Reef, Australia

12   Coral pool, southern edge of Heron Reef, Heron Island, Australia

13   Coral pool, southern edge of Heron Reef, Heron Island, Australia

14   Valerie's Reef with pink sea fans, Komodo Island, Indonesia

15   Valerie & Ewa, Heron Island-over/under, Great Barrier Reef, Australia

16   Valerie and Jonathon Heighes, her nephew, with gray nurse shark, *Carcharias taurus*, Seal Rocks, NSW, Australia

17   Valerie's nephew Mark and his friend Lena, Tikopea, Solomon Islands

18   Pacific bottlenose dolphins, *Tursiops truncatus*, South Australia

19   Ron and yellow crinoid, *Comanthina nobilis*, Marion Reef, Coral Sea

21   Invertebrate bouquet, Pink Sand Beach, Komodo Island, Indonesia

22   Ascidian colony, *Aplidium* sp., Pink Sand Beach, Komodo Island, Indonesia

23   Ascidian bouquet, *Polycarpa aurata*, Pink Sand Beach, Komodo Island, Indonesia

24   Posy of ascidians, stinging hydroids, and algae, Pink Sand Beach, Komodo Island, Indonesia

24   Nudibranchs, *Chromodoris* sp., Qatar, Arabian Gulf

25   Neon triplefin, *Helcogramma striata*, Pink Sand Beach, Komodo Island, Indonesia

26   Nudibranch, *Casella atromarginata*, Pink Sand Beach, Komodo Island, Indonesia

27   Nudibranch, *Chromodoris westraliensis*, Mai Island, Luci Para Islands, Banda Sea, Indonesia

27   Fire urchin, *Astonosoma intermedium*, Pink Sand Beach, Komodo Island, Indonesia

28   Nudibranchs, *Chromodoris* sp., Doha Island, Qatar, Arabian Gulf

28   Nudibranchs, *Chromodoris lochi*, Luci Para Islands, Banda Sea, Indonesia

29   Nudibranchs, *Chromodoris bullocki*, Banda Island, Banda Sea, Indonesia

31   Saddleback butterflyfish, *Chaetodon ephippium*, Heron Island, Great Barrier Reef, Australia

32   Bridled parrotfish, *Scarus frenatus*, Heron Island, southern Great Barrier Reef, Australia

32   Bluebarred parrotfish, *Scarus ghobban*, with tubesta coral, Heron Island Bommie, southern Great Barrier Reef, Australia

33   Parrotfish, *Scarus gibbus*, Heron Island Bommie, Great Barrier Reef, Australia

34   Titan triggerfish, *Balistoides viridescens*, Port Sudan, Red Sea

35   Tomato rockcod, *Cephalopholis sonnerati*, Milne Bay, Papua New Guinea

36   Silhouetted batfish, *Platax teira*, Walindi Plantation, Kimbe Bay, Papua New Guinea

36   Schooling batfish, *Platax teira*, Lady Elliot Island, Great Barrier Reef, Australia

37   Crocodilefish, *Cymbacephalus beauforti*, Pink Sand Beach, Komodo Island, Indonesia

38   Harlequin tuskfish, *Choerodon fasciatus*, Wistari Reef, Capricorn Banker Group, Great Barrier Reef, Australia

39   Harlequin tuskfish, *Choerodon fasciatus*, southern Great Barrier Reef, Australia

41   Schooling shrimpfish, *Aeoliscus strigatus*, Milne Bay, Papua New Guinea

42   Frogfish, *Antennarius maculatus*, Observation Point, Milne Bay, Papua New Guinea

42   Sculptured toadfish, *Halophryne queenslandiae*, Heron Island, Great Barrier Reef, Australia

43   Giant frogfish, *Antennarius commersoni*, Ambon, Indonesia

44   Tomato anemonefish, *Premnas biaculeatus*, Milne Bay, Papua New Guinea

45   Snorkeler with whale shark, *Rhincodon typus*, Ningaloo Reef, Exmouth, northwestern Australia

46   Cheeklined Maori wrasse, *Cheilinus digrammus*, Shaab Rumi, Red Sea

46   Cheeklined Maori wrasse, *Cheilinus digrammus*, Shaab Rumi, Red Sea

47   Cheeklined Maori wrasse, *Cheilinus digrammus*, Shaab Rumi, Red Sea

47   Cheeklined Maori wrasse, *Cheilinus digrammus*, Shaab Rumi, Red Sea

48   School of pufferfish, *Arothron nigropunctatus*, Sydney, Australia

48   Dussumier's surgeonfish, *Acanthurus dussumieri*, Luci Para Islands, Banda Sea, Indonesia

49   Unicorn surgeonfish, *Naso brevirostris*, Raine Island, Great Barrier Reef, Australia

49   Ghost pipefish, *Solenostomus paradoxus*, Banda Island, Banda Sea, Indonesia

50   Black tuskfish and cleaner wrasse, *Choerodon schoeleinii* and *Labroides dimidiatus*, Heron Island Bommie, Australia

50   Juvenile batfish, *Platax batavianus*, Milne Bay, Papua New Guinea

51   Chevron barracuda, *Sphyraena putnamiae*, Walindi Plantation, Kimbe Bay, Papua New Guinea

53   Great white shark, *Carcharodon carcharias*, Dangerous Reef, South Australia

54   Great white shark, *Carcharodon carcharias*, Dangerous Reef, South Australia

57   Great white shark, *Carcharodon carcharias*, Dangerous Reef, South Australia

58   Great white shark, *Carcharodon carcharias*, South Neptune Island, South Australia

63   Great white shark, *Carcharodon carcharias*, South Neptune Island, South Australia

65   Valerie's Rock, Komodo Island, Indonesia

66   Valerie's Rock, Komodo Island, Indonesia

67   Soft coral, *Dendronephthya* sp., Great Barrier Reef, Australia

69   Corals and sponges in sea cave, Luci Para Islands, Indonesia

70   Yellow-orange soft coral, *Dendronephthya* sp., Luci Para Islands, Indonesia

71   Coral polyp, *Trachypora lacera*, Heron Island, Great Barrier Reef, Australia

72   Soft corals, *Sarcophyton trocheliophorum*, Heron Island, Great Barrier Reef, Australia

73   Elegant hard coral, *Pectinia paeonia*, Heron Island, Great Barrier Reef, Australia

74   Leather coral, *Dendronephthya* sp., Heron Island, Great Barrier Reef, Australia

75   Pink brittle star on pink soft coral, *Ophiothrix purpurea/Dendronephthya* sp., Banda Island, Indonesia

76   Spawning coral polyps, *Acropora* sp., Heron Island, Great Barrier Reef, Australia

77   Jellyfish, *Phyllorhiza punctata*, East Coast, Australia

78   Reef scene with crinoids, Valerie's Reef, Komodo, Indonesia

79   Galápagos sea lion, *Zalophus californianus wollebaeki*, San Salvador Island, Galápagos

81   Australian sea lions, *Neophoca cinerea*, Hopkins Island, South Australia

84   Australian sea lions, *Neophoca cinerea*, Hopkins Island, South Australia

85   Ron filming Australian sea lions, *Neophoca cinerea*, Hopkins Island, South Australia

88/9 Australian sea lions, *Neophoca cinerea*, Hopkins Island, South Australia

91   Great white swimming toward surface, *Carcharodon carcharias*, Dangerous Reef, South Australia

92   Great white shark, *Carcharodon carcharias*, Dangerous Reef, South Australia

95   Great white shark, *Carcharodon carcharias*, Dangerous Reef, South Australia

96   Ron filming whale shark, *Rhincodon typus*, Ningaloo Reef, Exmouth, Western Australia

97   Whale shark with pilot fish, *Rhincodon typus*, Ningaloo Reef, Exmouth, Western Australia

98/9 Snorkeler with whale shark, *Rhincodon typus*, Ningaloo Reef, Exmouth, Western Australia

101   Kathy Trout, Turtle Island, Fiji

102   Native boy spearfishing, Trobriand Islands, Papua New Guinea

103   Tove Peterson, Banda Sea, Indonesia

106   Valerie and potato cod, *Epinephelus tukula*, Cod Hole, Comerant Pass, Great Barrier Reef (photographed by Greg Heighes)

108   Sleeping loggerhead turtle, *Caretta caretta*, wreck of the *Yongala*, Townsville, Queensland, Australia

109   Baby loggerhead turtle, *Caretta caretta*, Great Barrier Reef, Australia

109   Sleeper or nurse shark with turtle, *Nebrius ferrugineus*, Raine Island, Great Barrier Reef, Australia

110   Green turtles, *Chelonia mydas*, Heron Island, Great Barrier Reef, Australia

111   Loggerhead turtle, *Caretta caretta*, Heron Island, Great Barrier Reef, Australia

113   Valerie in mesh suit, San Diego, California

115   Blue shark, *Prionace glauca*, San Diego, California

116   Ron and Valerie with blue shark, *Prionace glauca*, San Diego, California

118   Valerie with blue shark, *Prionace glauca*, San Diego, California

121   In the chasm in Picininney Ponds, Picininney Chasm, South Australia

122   Banded octopus, *Octopus horrida*, Observation Point, Milne Bay, Papua New Guinea

123   Turtle-headed sea snake, *Emydocephalus annulatus*, Swain Reefs, Coral Sea

124   Marbled ray, *Taeniura meyeri*, Cocos Island, Costa Rica

124   Shark ray, *Rhina ancylostoma*, Sydney, New South Wales, Australia

125   Juvenile flying fish, *Exocoetidae* sp., Low Island, Great Barrier Reef, Australia

125   Shortbodied blenny, *Exallias brevis*, Luci Para Islands, Banda Sea, Indonesia

126   Blue-ringed octopus, *Hapalochlaena lunulata*, Spencers Gulf, South Australia

126   Nudibranch, *Melibe mirifica*, Observation Point, Milne Bay, Papua New Guinea

126   Flamboyant cuttlefish, *Metasepia pfeifferi*, Observation Point, Milne Bay, Papua New Guinea

127   Leafy sea dragon, *Phycodurus eques*, Spencers Gulf, South Australia

128   Australian giant cuttlefish, *Sepia apama*, Banda Island, Banda Sea, Indonesia

129   Cleaner shrimp, *Hippolysmata grabhami*, Milne Bay, Papua New Guinea

129   Feeding sea apple cucumber, *Pseudocolochirus axiologus*, Milne Bay, Papua New Guinea

130   Wentletrap, *Epitoniidae* sp., Heron Island Bommie, Great Barrier Reef, Australia

130   Shrimp, *Saron* sp., Mai Island, Luci Para Islands, Banda Sea, Indonesia

131   Hermit crab, *Calliactis polypus*, Milne Bay, Papua New Guinea

132   Jellyfish, *Thysanostoma thysanura*, Seal Rocks, New South Wales, Australia

133   Nautilus, *Nautilus scrobiculatus*, New Britain, Papua New Guinea

135   Great hammerhead shark, *Sphyrna mokarran*, Swain Reefs, Coral Sea

136   Gray nurse shark, *Carcharium taurus*, Seal Rocks, New South Wales, Australia

138   Tiger shark, *Galeocerdo cuvier*, Coralita Pass, Marion Reef, Coral Sea

141   Gray nurse shark, *Carcharias taurus*, Manly Oceanarium, Sydney, Australia

142   Tawny or nurse shark, *Nebrius concolor*, Raine Island, northern Great Barrier Reef, Australia

145   Silvertip shark with jacks, *Carcharhinus albimarginatus*, Moore Reef, Coral Sea

146   Leopard shark, *Stegostoma fasciatum*, Lady Elliot Island, southern Great Barrier Reef, Australia

148   Christiana Carvalho freediving, Luci Para Islands, Banda Sea, Indonesia

149   Redfin anthias, *Pseudanthias dispar*, Komodo Island, Indonesia

150   Red-and-white tubeworms, *Silogranella* sp., Luci Para Islands, Banda Sea, Indonesia

151   Red firefish, *Pterois volitans*, Milne Bay, Papua New Guinea

153   Great white shark, *Carcharodon carcharias*, caught in mesh net, Gold Coast, southern Queensland, Australia

154   Valerie in the cave full of orange corals, Luci Para Islands, Banda Sea, Indonesia

159   Whitetip reef shark, *Triaenodon obesus*, Osprey Reef, Coral Sea

The shark may not love as we do, but the tenderness of this courting male as he woos his larger companion is obvious. Matching her movements he touches her gently, as a lover would. I was a privileged observer from another world, neither welcome nor unwanted but simply ignored. I am indeed the most fortunate of women, for I have seen beneath the surface, beyond the painting on the canvas, into the private soul of the sea.

PUBLISHER
Fourth Day Publishing, Inc.
San Antonio, Texas

EXECUTIVE EDITOR
Cheryl Schorp
San Antonio, Texas

DESIGN
Charlene deJori
San Antonio, Texas

COLOR & PRINTING
Dynagraphics, Inc.
Portland, Oregon